Cambridge Elements ≡

Elements in Perception
edited by
James T. Enns
The University of British Columbia

THE PERVASIVENESS OF ENSEMBLE PERCEPTION

Not Just Your Average Review

Jennifer E. Corbett
The Ohio State University

Igor Utochkin
University of Chicago

Shaul Hochstein
The Hebrew University of Jerusalem

CAMBRIDGE
UNIVERSITY PRESS

Shaftesbury Road, Cambridge CB2 8EA, United Kingdom

One Liberty Plaza, 20th Floor, New York, NY 10006, USA

477 Williamstown Road, Port Melbourne, VIC 3207, Australia

314–321, 3rd Floor, Plot 3, Splendor Forum, Jasola District Centre,
New Delhi – 110025, India

103 Penang Road, #05–06/07, Visioncrest Commercial, Singapore 238467

Cambridge University Press is part of Cambridge University Press & Assessment,
a department of the University of Cambridge.

We share the University's mission to contribute to society through the pursuit of
education, learning and research at the highest international levels of excellence.

www.cambridge.org
Information on this title: www.cambridge.org/9781009222709

DOI: 10.1017/9781009222716

First published 2023

A catalogue record for this publication is available from the British Library.

ISBN 978-1-009-22270-9 Paperback
ISSN 2515-0502 (online)
ISSN 2515-0499 (print)

Cambridge University Press & Assessment has no responsibility for the persistence
or accuracy of URLs for external or third-party internet websites referred to in this
publication and does not guarantee that any content on such websites is, or will
remain, accurate or appropriate.

The Pervasiveness of Ensemble Perception

Not Just Your Average Review

Elements in Perception

DOI: 10.1017/9781009222716
First published online: January 2023

Jennifer E. Corbett
The Ohio State University

Igor Utochkin
University of Chicago

Shaul Hochstein
The Hebrew University of Jerusalem

Author for correspondence: Jennifer E. Corbett, jennifer.e.corbett@gmail.com

Abstract: This Element outlines the recent understanding of ensemble representations in perception in a holistic way aimed to engage the general audience, novice and expert alike. The Element highlights the ubiquitous nature of this summary process, paving the way for a discussion of the theoretical and cortical underpinnings, and why ensemble encoding should be considered a basic, inherently necessary component of human perception. Following an overview of the topic, including a brief history of the field, the Element introduces overarching themes and a corresponding outline of the present work.

Keywords: ensemble encoding, perceptual averaging, summary statistical representation, gist perception, contextual vision

ISBNs: 9781009222709 (PB), 9781009222716 (OC)
ISSNs: 2515-0502 (online), 2515-0499 (print)

Contents

1 Introduction and Scope

The human visual system can only access detailed representations of a fraction of information in each glance, with the heuristic limit of about four items. This raises the questions of what happens to the remaining majority of visual input, and why we nonetheless have the illusion of stable and complete perception? Ensemble representations are rapidly extracted statistical summaries of sets of similar items. For example, without individuating leaves in Figure 1a, an immediate impression of Summer versus Autumn is given by average hue. Similarly, it is not necessary to encode individual trees in Figure 1b to understand one forest has grown naturally and one has been planted based on variance in size and position.

1.1 Brief History

In vision science, ensemble encoding is synonymous with summary statistical representation, or encoding sets of objects in terms of statistical descriptors versus detailed individual representations. Although multiple statistical properties of ensembles can be represented, the majority of investigations to date have been concerned with mean representations, often termed "perceptual averaging." Importantly, "ensemble" has different meaning in these contexts than in mathematics and machine learning, where ensemble methods involve evaluating multiple models to maximize prediction accuracy. The term ensemble in vision science was likely inherited from the texture perception literature, referring to a collection of items in which each part is only considered with respect to the whole.

Ariely (2001) popularized ensemble encoding with a foundational demonstration that although observers were at chance to determine whether a circle presented after a set of circles was a member of the set, they were surprisingly accurate at discriminating whether it was larger than the average size of the set. Since then, a number of tasks have been developed to characterize ensemble perception either by explicitly measuring mean representation or by implicitly probing the effect of task-irrelevant mean information on performance (Figure 2). Yet, phenomena of central tendency were long before central topics in perception. Representing parts with respect to wholes is a major tenet underlying Gestalt principles (Wertheimer, 1923). Even before the formalization of Gestalt laws, the idea that "the whole is more than the sum of its parts," was deeply rooted in empirical studies of number perception. Messenger (1903) reported observers were poor at discriminating how many objects comprised a set of radially arranged lines but became more accurate after drawing the stimulus from memory, suggesting elements were encoded relative to the whole set. Similarly, the idea that perception "regresses toward the mean" is evident in early empirical studies of human information processing. Hollingworth (1910)

a b

Figure 1 (a) Differences in average hue allow for rapid perception of different seasons in Summer (top) and Autumn (bottom) leaves. (b) Lower size and position variance allow for quick discrimination between natural (top) and human-made (bottom) forests.

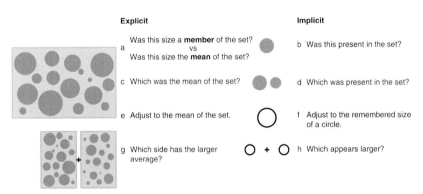

Figure 2 Typical explicit (left) and implicit (right) tasks used to investigate ensemble perception. (a) Observers can explicitly determine whether a test represents the set mean but not whether it was a member of the set, and (b) show implicit bias to incorrectly choose circles closer to the mean as set members. (c) Observers can explicitly determine which test was the set mean, but (d) are implicitly biased toward incorrectly selecting the mean as a member present in the set. (e) Observers can explicitly adjust a test to the mean, but (f) adjustments for set members are implicitly biased toward the mean. (g) Observers can explicitly determine which side has the larger mean, but (h) after adapting to two sets with different means, perceptions of physically identical tests are implicitly biased as an inverse function of the mean.

presented observers with a square for approximately five seconds, then asked them to choose which of several squares matched its size. He noted the "indifference point" or mean value around which estimates tended to gravitate. Attneave (1954) proposed the visual system behaves like an intuitive statistician, averaging out redundancy and retaining abstract statistical regularities. Along these lines, Barlow (1961) noted early visual neurons extract signals of high relative entropy out of largely redundant visual input, emphasizing the unusual by summarizing regularities. See Bauer (2015) for a comprehensive review of "pre-Ariely" studies.

1.2 Themes and Outline

Over the course of summarizing what has been uncovered about ensemble representation, we will develop the following themes in this Element. In Section 2, we aim to provide succinct descriptions of fundamental results that are often overgeneralized to aid in the interpretation of existing literature and guide the development of future investigations. In Section 3, we review several theoretical questions regarding ensemble encoding and propose it is best understood in terms of Reverse Hierarchy Theory (RHT; Hochstein & Ahissar, 2002). This is followed in Section 4 by a discussion of the corresponding computational and neural substrates of ensemble encoding. In contrast to leading views, we propose in Section 5 that ensemble encoding does not supplement focused attentional processing, but instead is a more fundamental process. We point out how perception is reliant on ensemble summaries without the need to retrieve noisy individual representations when processing capacity is exceeded, but not at the expense of fidelity when details can be recovered via focused attention with minimal corruption. Our overarching conclusion is that ensemble perception is the basis of a qualitatively different, intelligent form of representation and the starting point of conscious perception giving rise to our remarkable abilities to organize huge chunks of sensory information and maintain a holistic "big picture" with the illusion of detail.

2 What Is Summarized?

Before turning to advanced discussions, it is important to review foundational studies of the spatial, temporal, multimodal, and statistical properties of ensemble representations. While the seasoned reader may opt to skip to later sections, here we provide expert and novice readers alike with sufficient detail to properly interpret the implications of seminal works and to optimize the design of future studies of ensemble encoding.

2.1 Features

So far, it seems anything can be summarized in an ensemble representation. In fact, there has never been an empirical demonstration that summary representations can be prevented. Here we discuss an abbreviated list of fundamental demonstrations of ensemble encoding over an array of features.

2.1.1 Size

Ariely's (2001) investigation launched the now-popular proposal that sets of objects can be represented in a qualitatively different manner than individual objects. Subsequent studies by Chong and Treisman demonstrated observers could discriminate which of two sets of heterogeneously sized circles had the larger average size with similar precision as they could determine which of two displays of homogeneous circles or which of two single circles was larger, and average estimates were unaffected by display duration (2003), density, or set size (2005a). However, it is important to note here and in many studies discussed throughout this work that only four unique sizes were used in their displays. Therefore, observers may have relied on individual representations of the unique sizes without necessitating a specialized averaging process. These findings do align with earlier reports that estimates of average length and tilt of sets of six lines followed Stevens' Power Law, with one-to-one relationships between physical and perceived properties (Miller & Sheldon, 1969; Miller et al., 1970; Weiss & Anderson, 1969).

2.1.2 Orientation

Foundational work in texture perception has also noted the visual system's basic ability to average orientations. Dakin and colleagues (Dakin, 1997; Dakin & Watt, 1997) presented the first empirical evidence that observers were able to discriminate the mean orientation of sets of 512 elements and parse the mean orientations of subsets of 64 element displays with similar precision as reported for single orientation discriminations.

2.1.3 Speed/Direction of Motion

Williams and Sekuler (1984) first noted global coherent motion was perceived in the direction of the mean trajectory of random dot kinematograms. Watamaniuk and colleagues (1989) then demonstrated mean direction is perceived without regard for individual dot paths, and discrimination thresholds for dots moving at different speeds were similar to thresholds for dots moving at the same speed (Watamaniuk & Duchon (1992).

2.1.4 Brightness

Bauer (2009) reported Stevens' Power Law extended to average brightness with displays of sixteen circles with four unique luminances. Takano and Kimura (2020) recently reported discriminations of the average brightness of six to twelve discs were as or more precise than discriminations of individual disc brightness.

2.1.5 Color

When briefly presented with eight squares, half in one hue and half in a different hue, observers were more likely to incorrectly select a square matching the mean hue as being present versus a hue that was present (Maule et al., 2014). These findings corroborate Olkkonen and colleagues' (2014) report that observers' perceptions of individual hues in a delayed estimation task were biased toward the set mean, as well as Webster and colleagues (2014) findings that observers could accurately estimate the average hue of 121 elements with half presented in one hue and the other half presented in a second hue.

2.1.6 Location

Using a multiple object tracking task with an attended set of four identical targets and an unattended set of four different identical targets, Alvarez and Oliva (2008) found not only were participants more accurate at indicating the centroid location of the attended set versus the location of an individual attended object, but they also encoded the mean versus individual locations of the unattended set. Lew and Vul (2013) subsequently found observers recalled individual locations more accurately when two to eight objects were densely clustered versus individually distributed, and judgments had lower absolute errors relative to the centroid location of the entire cluster versus individual item locations (Lew & Vul, 2015).

2.1.7 Numerosity

Solomon and Morgan (2018) presented observers with two displays of four or eight "sectors," each occupied by zero to four items, and asked them to judge which display contained the larger average numerosity. Judgments were similar for displays when items occupied both equal and unequal numbers of sectors, suggesting calculations of average versus total numerosity.

2.1.8 Numeric Value

Corbett and colleagues (2006) first demonstrated rapid extraction of a higher-order, meaningful stimulus property, average numeric value. Observers viewed two briefly presented displays of mixtures of six block 2's and 5's (digits condition), p's and q's (letters condition), and displays rotated by 90° (sideways digits and sideways letters conditions), and judged which display had the larger average value (digits), more of a given target letter (letters) or target shape (sideways conditions). Digit judgments were significantly faster and more accurate, suggesting observers rapidly extracted average numeric value when it was meaningful in digits displays in a qualitatively different manner than when evaluating which meaningful letter display or which nonmeaningful rotated displays contained more of a given target. Later studies by Brezis and colleagues confirmed averaging of large sequences of two-digit numbers (2015, 2016, 2018).

2.1.9 Faces

Haberman and Whitney (2007) demonstrated perceptual averaging of meaningful, high-level face stimuli. Observers determined whether a test face was happier than a set of four faces with different emotional expressions about as accurately as they determined whether the test was happier than a set of homogeneous-expression faces, but could not determine which of two faces was a member of a set of four different-expression faces. Results replicated for average gender, and held over displays of upright but not inverted or scrambled faces with larger set sizes (8, 12, and 16 faces comprised four unique faces), regardless of poor location memory for individual members and whether sets were displayed for 50 ms or 2 s (Haberman & Whitney, 2009). De Fockert and Wolfenstein (2009) also reported observers were more likely to incorrectly select the mean identity of a set of four unfamiliar faces as present versus an individual identity that was present. This finding was later replicated for sets of four familiar famous faces (Neumann et al., 2013), and four exemplars of the same celebrity regardless of simultaneous or sequential presentation (Kramer et al., 2015).

2.1.10 Biological Factors

Sweeny and Whitney (2014) reported observers were able to accurately estimate the average perceived eye gaze direction of sets of up to four faces regardless of whether sets were presented for 200 or 1000 ms. This effect attenuated with inverted faces, suggesting both low-level features and higher-level configural information are statistically summarized. Observers were also able to accurately estimate the heading of a crowd of two to twelve point-light-walkers with unique individual trajectories, with precision increasing as a function of set size (Sweeny et al., 2013). Yamanashi Leib and colleagues (2016) reported observers were able to accurately estimate the average animacy of a set of six objects when the entire set was briefly presented and when individual objects were presented in succession.

2.1.11 Category

Khayat and Hochstein (2019) presented observers with Rapid Serial Visual Presentation (RSVP) displays of nine or twelve objects from the same category (e.g., mammals) and asked them to choose which of two tests were present. Observers were faster and more accurate to choose the prototypical test over a nonprototypical test or a different category test. Findings also extended to novel "amoeba" shapes (Khayat et al., 2021).

2.1.12 Economic Value

A recent study by Yamanashi Leib and colleagues (2020) showed observers made fairly accurate average price estimates of sets of up to six different retail products (e.g., microwave, backpack, shoe, lamp, bowl, t-shirt).

2.1.13 Temporal

Kanaya and colleagues (2018) reported mean frequency estimates for sets of up to fourteen different frequencies were biased toward the most salient (highest) frequency (see Section 3.3.3), in line with previous reports of temporal distortion induced by rhythmic timing (Johnston et al., 2006). Furthermore, observers perceived the duration of a test dot as an inverse function of the average dot duration of a stream of eleven different-duration adapting dots, suggesting average duration is encoded as a fundamental property of visual information (Corbett et al., 2021).

These findings converge to suggest ensemble encoding is ubiquitous in visual information processing, with automatic averaging of a large variety of low- and high-level features. Although truly categorical variables (e.g., apples and oranges) are inherently unavailable to averaging, ensemble encoding is so pervasive that perhaps all features can be summarized in an exemplar form.

2.2 Modalities

2.2.1 Auditory

Ensemble representation is not limited to visual features. In fact, Albrecht and colleagues (2012) demonstrated when participants viewed sequences of serially presented eight circles with different sizes and/or heard sequences of eight serially presented tones with different pitches and were tasked either to adjust a subsequent tone to the average pitch or a circle to the average size, adjustments were significantly more accurate for average tone than size regardless of whether circles and tones were presented simultaneously. Along these lines, listeners were remarkably accurate when presented with six tones in sequence and asked to determine whether the mean frequency was higher than a test tone but unable to discriminate whether the mean or a foil was present in the set or an individual tone's sequence in the set (Piazza et al., 2013). Schweickert and colleagues (2014) reported similar findings for tone duration when listeners were presented with sets of forty tones sampled from different durations and asked to determine whether a comparison tone was longer than the set average. McDermott and colleagues (2013) presented listeners with three different auditory textures (e.g., stream, insects, fire) and asked them to determine which sound was generated from a distinct source. Performance improved as texture duration increased with two exemplars from one texture and one exemplar from a different texture, but declined with increasing duration with two identical exemplars and a third exemplar from a different excerpt of the same texture (identical long-term statistics, with different temporal details in the unique texture). Collectively, results suggest temporal details are summarized using time-averaged statistics which converge for the same sounds over increasing durations.

2.2.2 Perception and Action

Investigations of ensemble encoding in perception and action have so far yielded mixed results. When Corbett and Song (2014) adapted observers to two arrays of fourteen differently sized circles, they perceived a test circle as larger when presented in the region adapted to the smaller versus larger mean size (a negative adaptation aftereffect; AAE). However, when observers were asked to grasp the 2D test circle, actions were initially biased in line with the perceptual aftereffect but corrected over the course of the action. In a later study by Fan and colleagues (2021) using veridical 3D haptic feedback, manual estimations of the size or orientation of a 3D cylindrical target surrounded by elliptical and cylindrical objects were biased by both the mean orientation and mean size of the entire display, but peak grasping apertures to the 3D target were not. Similarly, when presented with a single target and asked to adjust a line to estimate its size or reach to grasp it, estimates were biased toward the most frequently presented size over subsequent trials but peak grip apertures were not influenced regardless of visual feedback (Hamidi et al., 2021).

2.3 Timing

In addition to representing sets of objects arranged in space, several studies have investigated how ensembles are encoded over time. Such investigations have measured the temporal dynamics of simultaneously presented displays, as well as ensemble encoding of sequentially presented individual items.

2.3.1 Timescale of Simultaneous Encoding

Whereas early findings suggested ensemble encoding happens almost instantaneously, there is mounting evidence this process occurs over a slightly longer time scale. Chong and Treisman (2003) first reported observers could discriminate which of two side-by-side displays of twelve circles (four unique sizes) had the larger average size with presentation durations as fast as 50 ms. In line with these findings, Li and colleagues (2016) presented observers with sets of four faces for 50 ms, 500 ms, 1,000 ms, 1,500 ms, or 2,000 ms and asked them to judge whether a subsequently presented test face was a member of the set or more neutral than the set mean. Mean discriminations were similarly accurate across exposure durations for homogeneous and heterogeneous sets, whereas longer exposure times were needed for accurate member discriminations. Together, results suggested averages, but not individual representations, can be extracted as quickly as 50 ms. However, Whiting and Oriet (2011) demonstrated when displays are immediately masked to delimit processing, durations of at least 200 ms were necessary for comparably accurate mean size discriminations. Similarly, when successively presented with two random dot kinematograms, the difference in global motion necessary for observers to discriminate whether the global motion of the second stimulus was left or right of the global motion asymptoted around 465 ms (Watamaniuk & Sekuler, 1992). Results collectively imply ensemble representations are rapidly extracted within a temporal integration window of at least 200 ms. Given considerable methodological variance, this window likely depends on multiple factors, including feature(s), task, and temporal dynamics.

2.3.2 Over Time

In addition to investigating the temporal dynamics of simultaneously presented ensembles, a number of studies have measured ensemble encoding over successively presented items. Chong and Treisman (2005a) presented observers with a sequence of eight circles (four unique sizes), each for 250 ms, and found a difference of about 22 percent was necessary to discriminate which of two probes corresponded to the mean size, but a difference of approximately 45 percent was necessary to determine which probe corresponded to given set member. Haberman and colleagues (2009) presented observers with sets of four to twenty faces (four unique faces) at different temporal frequencies and asked them either to judge whether a test face was more disgusted than the average expression or to adjust a face to the average expression. Based on decay function fits to performance over durations, sets needed to be presented for approximately 800 ms to reach 63 percent of an asymptotic performance threshold. Inaccurate temporal order judgments for single faces were taken as evidence that individual faces were not reliably encoded, yet item order cannot usually be retained from RSVP sequences (e.g., Hommel & Akyürek, 2005). Therefore, observers in both studies may have responded based on individual representations. Corbett and Oriet (2011) first demonstrated size averaging over RSVP displays of five to eleven uniquely sized circles. These findings were later replicated using larger set sizes of all or mostly unique objects for average size, orientation, and brightness (Khayat & Hochstein, 2018), identity (Yamanashi-Leib et al., 2014), animacy (Yamanashi Leib, 2016), and familiar (Khayat & Hochstein, 2019) and novel (Khayat et al., 2021) object categories.

Although ensembles are clearly represented over time, it is less understood whether all items contribute equally. When Weiss and Anderson (1969) presented observers with a sequence of six lines with different lengths, each for 4 s with a 2 s Inter-stimulus interval (ISI), then asked them to adjust a test line to the mean length, adjustments were biased toward later lengths. Albrecht and Scholl (2010) found a similar recency bias in mean size adjustments when observers were presented with one disc that size-morphed over 720 ms and remained in the same spatial position, moved randomly through nine anchor points, or a set of eight discs that remained in the same spatial locations but size-morphed over 1.2 s. When the disc changed at a linear rate, estimates reflected overall mean size, but when half of the transformation happened five times faster, adjustments were biased toward the size in the longer half. Average estimates were also influenced more by expanding versus contracting portions of the sequence. Tong and colleagues (2019) also reported a recency effect for the average length of a one-second series of individually presented lines and to a lesser extent the running average of a sequence of numerals, suggesting recency bias varies over different features. Somewhat to the contrary, Hubert-Wallander and Boynton (2015) reported although mean size, facial expression, and direction of motion exhibited recency effects, the average location of a stream of serially presented objects was biased toward earlier items. This primacy bias is similar to later findings by Crawford and colleagues (2019) that observers' current average of four squares or emotional faces simultaneously presented for 1 s were biased toward the mean value of the previous display. When presented with a disc that continuously changed size at different rates and asked to adjust a test to match the mean size, Attarha and colleagues (2016) reported observers' estimates were fairly constant and accurate for durations up to about 600 ms, pointing to a limited temporal window for integration with all items contributing equally, such that representations are not continuously but rather periodically updated.

Collectively, findings demonstrate ensemble representations are accrued over both time and space, and further suggest ensemble encoding may be modulated by the temporal saliency of individual items. As discussed further in Section 5.4, periodically updating summary representations of the dynamic surrounding environment may provide a critical mechanism to mediate between the needs to perceive salient changes while maintaining the impression of stable, complete perception.

2.4 Statistical Descriptors

Although the ability to extract average features from a set of multiple objects is a signature phenomenon of ensemble perception, computation of summary statistics is not limited to the mean. In other words, the representation of a set is not compressed into a single representative magnitude, but instead into an ensemble of useful statistical descriptors.

2.4.1 Numerosity

Numerosity, an immediate approximation of quantity without counting, is another statistical property extracted in parallel over a set of objects (Chong & Evans, 2011). Although the number of discrete objects is different from an average feature, some authors suggest the actual visual property underlying numerosity is relative texture density (e.g., Durgin, 1995, 2008; Section 2.5.3). However, others argue numerosity is more than just texture density (Burr & Ross, 2008) reliant upon an independent neural substrate. In any case, numerosity perception shares critical properties of ensemble summary statistics in that it is an approximate, gist-based representation that can be rapidly accessed.

2.4.2 Variability

Sensitivity to set variance or range has been documented using paradigms similar to those outlined for averaging tasks over various domains, such as orientation (e.g., Lau & Brady, 2018; Tokita et al., 2016), brightness (Khayat & Hochstein, 2018) facial expression (Haberman et al., 2015). Solomon and colleagues (Morgan et al., 2008; Solomon, 2010) parametrically estimated sensitivity to orientation variance in a 2IFC task with displays of 121 gratings presented for 200 ms, separated by 200 ms blanks. Thresholds for determining which display had the greater variance were best described as "dipper function," which steadily increased with absolute variance over a broad range of physical variances, except for very small variances (up to 4–5°). Within this narrow range, discrimination thresholds instead decreased as variance increased, suggesting a threshold below which all variance is discounted as internal noise.

Variance and range also modulate the quality of average representations. The greater the variance, the more uncertain observers were about their judgments of average ensemble features (e.g., Corbett et al., 2012; Dakin, 2001; Im & Halberda, 2013; Maule & Franklin, 2015; Utochkin & Tiurina, 2014). Nonetheless, Hochstein and colleagues (2018) reported the mean orientations of two arrays of heterogeneously oriented bars were able to be compared even when ranges overlapped considerably, suggesting variability is an estimate of the external noise in the average representation. However, variability estimation has been demonstrated to transfer from a set with one average feature to a set with a different average feature (Haberman et al., 2015; Khvostov & Utochkin, 2019), suggesting relative independence between these two types of ensemble summaries (Section 3.1).

2.4.3 Distribution

The richness of ensemble representation also extends beyond basic summaries. In a series of experiments, Chetverikov and colleagues (2016, 2017a–c, 2019) demonstrated the entire feature distribution implicitly affects behavior. Participants searched for a feature-singleton among a large set of distractors. In streaks of 3–6 consecutive trials, distractors were drawn from the same distribution. Following the streak, the distractor distribution and target changed locations in feature space, such that the target could be one of the features within the former distractor distribution. This target-distractor reversal slowed search in a manner that correlated with the probability density of the probed feature in the previous distractor distribution, suggesting observers somehow learned the distractor distributions which negatively primed subsequent search. However, later work suggests only basic summary statistics (e.g., mean and variance) are consciously accessible, whereas observers cannot explicitly discriminate distractor sets with differently shaped distributions (Hansmann-Roth et al., 2021). Yet, Oriet and Hozempa (2016) showed observers can explicitly learn rich distributional properties from extended practice with a consistent feature distribution. Along these lines, Kim and Chong (2020) demonstrated observers rely on the whole feature distribution even when reporting only basic summary statistics, such that they tended to report the mean size of a sample set more precisely when other distributional properties of a test set matched those of the sample.

Ensemble representations are clearly not restricted to average properties but contain a rich array of descriptive information. Evidence discussed in the next section further suggests these properties are encoded as fundamental perceptual dimensions, directly accessed from ensembles versus built from individual parts using "vision-with-scrutiny."

2.5 Fundamental Nature

Implicit effects and lack of conscious awareness associated with ensemble representations raise the question of whether such representations are perceptual in nature. Are ensemble statistics immediately experienced as fundamental set properties, or inferred more "cognitively," based on single feature dimensions.

Strong evidence for the perceptual nature of ensemble statistical representations comes from studies of negative AAEs. As described in Section 2.2.2, after adapting to a given feature, perception of a test presented in the adapted region is biased in the opposite direction. Adaptation aftereffects (AAEs) are interpreted as evidence of basic perceptual encoding accomplished by a single mechanism comprised of independent units selectively sensitive over a limited range, such that units responsible for encoding one extreme become fatigued and the baseline response of units at the other extreme is falsely inflated (e.g., Campbell & Robson, 1968).

2.5.1 Size

Corbett and colleagues (2012) reported a robust AAE of mean size using adapting patches of fourteen dots on both sides from fixation with one patch always having a larger mean size (e.g., Figure 2h). Following adaptation, two test patches or dots were presented within the adapted regions. Observers' discriminations of which test had the larger mean or individual size were biased as an inverse function of the average size to which the region was adapted.

2.5.2 Variance

Norman and colleagues (2015) demonstrated an AAE to ensemble variance using a similar design. Observers adapted to sets of Gabors with high and low orientation variance, then determined which of two test patches had a higher variance. The typical negative AAE bias was observed even when there was little orientation similarity between adaptors and tests. However, Jeong and Chong (2020) failed to replicate this effect with large mean differences between adaptors and tests. Maule and Franklin (2020) reported transfer between features, such that adapting to a highly variable ensemble of colors lead to the underestimation of orientation variability.

2.5.3 Numerosity

Burr and Ross (2008) reported an exceptionally large numerosity AAE, with perception biased as much as three-fold. Despite additional experiments to dissociate numerosity effects from other variables such as area, density, and size (Burr & Ross, 2008), Durgin (2008) referred to earlier findings (Durgin, 1995, 2008; Durgin & Huk, 1997; Durgin & Proffitt, 1996) showing the numerosity AAE decreased for displays of high band-pass elements, suggesting properties like spatial frequency and density may better account for the observed effects without necessitating a specialized numerosity mechanism.

2.5.4 Duration

Corbett and colleagues (2021; Section 2.1.13) reported a similar AAE for the average duration of serially presented sets of items. Importantly, the finding that average temporal aspects of visual information are also encoded as fundamental properties provides a direct link between ensemble encoding in space and time. Further such explorations of spatiotemporal properties of ensemble perception are crucial to advance our understanding of how the limited capacity visual system continuously mediates between the illusion of stable perception amidst the chaos of the constantly changing retinal image (Section 5.4).

2.5.5 Development

In addition to evidence for the fundamental nature of ensemble encoding, such processing abilities may develop over time like other forms of summary representation (e.g., numerosity). For example, Zosh and colleagues (2011) found nine-month-old infants detect a 1:2 change in numerosity of either of two but not three intermingled groups of colored dots, suggesting ensemble numerosity was perceived for two sets, and a change to the superset of all dots was detected regardless of how many subsets were presented. Sweeny and colleagues (2015) similarly tested ensemble perception in four-to-five-year-old children by presenting them with drawings of trees with different size oranges and asking them to help a monkey find which tree had larger oranges overall. When comparing trees with eight oranges each (with four unique sizes), performance was slightly poorer for children and nearly perfect for adults, but when comparing trees with eight homogeneously sized oranges, accuracy was much lower for children. Finally, when the two trees had different numbers of oranges, accuracy for both groups was significantly better when the larger oranges were on the tree with more fruit, but still above chance when the tree with less fruit had the larger average size oranges. Although children's abilities to encode ensembles do develop somewhat over time, these findings demonstrate the fundamental nature of ensemble encoding, similar to other basic perceptual processes known to mature over time.

Overall, there is mounting evidence that ensemble properties are encoded fundamentally, as basic perceptual dimensions. Discussed further in Section 3, this fundamental nature suggests ensemble representations can be directly accessed, not recovered from constituent item representations or by explicitly combining information about the sum and total from lower-level stages of processing.

2.6 Limitations

Whereas ensemble representations are virtually unlimited in terms of what can be summarized, such summaries may be subject to processing limitations. Here we outline findings regarding whether multiple statistical summaries can be computed at the same time and with the same quality.

2.6.1 Different Sets

We first consider studies of encoding a given summary statistic for different subsets in the same display. Chong and Treisman (2005b) originally concluded the means of two sets could be computed in parallel, without cost. They briefly presented observers with displays of spatially intermixed sets of twelve green and twelve red circles (in different ratios of two unique sizes). Discriminations of which of two probe circles matched the average size of a given color set were similar regardless of whether color was pre-cued, as well as when only one of the color sets was presented. However, when Brand and colleagues (2012) revisited these findings, they found participants could have chosen the correct probe based on calculating the mean of the entire set. Using displays of all uniquely sized circles instead resulted in a consistent detriment when color was not pre-cued. These patterns of performance extended to higher-level features, such as the average emotions of subsets of faces defined by sex, and probed with test faces equidistant from the mean, eliminating the whole-set mean strategy. Luo and Zhao (2018) reported a similar two-set-limit for pre-cue effects when observers were presented with displays of up to eight sets of spatially inter-mixed circles and adjusted a probe to match a given colors' average size. However, subsets only included four individual objects, such that individual size may have been the delimiting factor. Together, results suggest observers can compute the two subset means of a given feature, but at a cost relative to computing the mean of the entire set or a single subset.

Oriet and Brand (2013) further demonstrated averaging over the entire set cannot be prevented. First, observers were presented with displays of one or two groups of six vertical lines of different lengths and one or two groups of six horizontal lines of different lengths for 200 ms, and instructed to pay attention only to one set, then indicate which side of the display had the larger average length for that set. Next, participants again were instructed to only pay attention to one set and given unlimited time to scrutinize displays and adjust the mean length of the relevant set on one side to match the mean size of that same set on the opposite side. Regardless of whether displays were presented briefly or with unlimited viewing time, estimates were affected by the mean size of the irrelevant set. Yildirim and colleagues (2018) provided converging evidence the overall mean is represented automatically and more efficiently than multiple subset means by demonstrating participants' estimations of whole set means of displays of two sets of eight circles were unaffected by pre-cues to represent the entire set mean or one subset, whereas subset means benefited from pre-cuing. Halberda and colleagues (2006) found similar results for numerosity using displays of up to thirty-five dots. Observers could accurately report the numerosities of two spatially intermixed subsets without pre-cues, but a pre-cue advantage emerged with three sets, and superset numerosity was represented regardless of pre-cuing. Based on significant increases in incorrect reports of a numerosity other than zero when more than two color subsets were present and the numerosity of an unpresented set was probed, Poltoratski and Xu (2013) proposed visual short-term memory (VSTM) capacity to represent about three different colors was likely the delimiting factor.

Convergent evidence of limited capacity for encoding the same summary statistic over multiple sets, and a superset advantage when encoding the same statistic over subsets is given by a series of studies in which observers were asked to calculate the averages of four sets of four objects each presented either simultaneously or sequentially. If capacity is limited, performance for simultaneous versus sequential presentations or when all four sets are repeated (effectively doubling processing time). Attarha and Moore (2014) found when observers were presented with four sets of four Gabors and asked to report the orientation of one patch that was tilted differently, accuracy was lower with simultaneous versus sequential presentation and highest when sets were presented twice. This simultaneous disadvantage disappeared when all four patches had homogeneous orientations and the task could be performed without having to compute averages of individual subsets. Results replicated for average size, with a superset advantage such that there was no difference in performance between simultaneous and sequential presentations for discriminations of whether a probe was larger than the mean size of the entire set of sixteen circles. This superset advantage was confirmed for orientation averaging in a subsequent study, with an additional demonstration that computing four different averages of four different sets was capacity-limited relative to comparing four single sizes or four patches of homogeneous sizes (Attarha & Moore, 2015a). Results collectively suggest a limited capacity for computing summary statistics for multiple sets, with a cost in precision compared to computing the same superset statistic.

2.6.2 Different Feature Dimensions

Unlike convergent evidence for limited capacity to extract the same summary statistic from multiple subsets, discrepant results have been reported from studies where observers are tasked to represent multiple features of the same set and different features from different sets in parallel.

Emmanouil and Treisman (2008) reported a cost for computing two different features within the same set and within different sets. First, observers viewed two sets of eight moving circles on either side of the display and discriminated which side had the larger average size or the faster average speed. One side contained circles with two fixed sizes and two fixed speeds in different proportions. The other side contained two circles with each size and speed level, but individual size and speed values varied to result in a difference of 6–36 percent between the mean size or speed of the opposite side. When size was pre-cued, participants needed a smaller difference between the two average sizes for 75 percent correct discriminations. However, there was no significant difference in thresholds for pre-cued average speed discriminations. Next, a pre-cue advantage for speed emerged with two sets of eight stationary circles and eight moving X's, such that size and speed were fixed to only one of two spatially intermixed sets. Importantly, sets were further delimited by whether they were moving, and there were twice as many sets and individual objects on either side. Finally, with two stationary sets with different features (circles and right-tilted lines) on either side, a pre-cue advantage was found for both size and orientation. Collectively, results were taken as evidence of a cost for parallel representation of one ensemble feature of one set and a different ensemble feature of another set, despite potential methodological issues.

Using a similar design, Yörük and Boduroglu (2020) found no cost of divided attention between average size and orientation of the same set. Observers viewed sets of twelve lines, with unique lengths and orientations, and adjusted a probe to match either the mean orientation or length. In a blocked design, the relevant dimension was either pre-cued at the start of the block of trials, or post-cued with an auditory cue after the set on each trial. Observers' errors for average size and orientation adjustments were not correlated in any condition, suggesting independent summaries were constructed in parallel for both features of the same set.

Results from a study by Huang (2015) also point toward limited capacity for parallel representation of multiple ensembles features. Observers viewed displays of either one red or green circle and one horizontal or vertical rectangle, one colored circle and a patch of sixteen horizontal and vertical rectangles, one oriented rectangle and sixteen red and green circles, or sixteen oriented rectangles and sixteen colored circles, then discriminated the horizontal/vertical orientation, red/green color, or the average orientation or color, respectively. Responses were more accurate when color or orientation was pre-cued. Findings were interpreted as evidence that encoding two different averages of two different sets is as demanding as encoding two different features of two single objects. However, as discussed further in Section 5.3, displays used extreme stimuli that may have unintentionally caused observers to segregate sets into red and green and horizontal and vertical, effectively increasing the number of sets to be summarized.

Attarha and Moore (2015b) used a simultaneous-sequential paradigm to examine whether different features could be averaged in parallel for different sets and for the same set. When observers were presented with four sets of four Gabors that varied in size and orientation, such that one set had a mean size that differed from the other three sets and a different set had a mean orientation that differed from the other three sets, they made significantly fewer correct responses with simultaneous compared to sequential presentation. However, when asked to discriminate only whether the overall average orientation was left or right, the overall size was larger than a probe, or 4AFC regarding both average size and orientation, they performed similarly regardless of whether displays were presented simultaneously, sequentially, or twice. This superset advantage suggests capacity limitations for summarizing two different dimensions for each of four subsets relative to summarizing two different dimensions extracted parallel from the same set.

Overall, results tend to support the proposal that different ensemble features can be extracted from the same set in parallel, but there is limited capacity for simultaneously extracting one ensemble feature from one set and a different ensemble feature from another. Interestingly, Albrecht and colleagues (2012; Section 2.2.1) found no cost for simultaneously representing the average sizes of a set of circles and the average pitch of a sequence of tones. However, given the overall superior performance for auditory averaging, it is possible visual and auditory streams were represented separately even when presented simultaneously. Future studies using methods developed by Attarha and Moore (2015b) and Yörük and Boduroglu (2020) may help to determine whether ensembles can be represented in parallel over multiple modalities.

2.6.3 Multiple Descriptors

A handful of studies have considered how ensemble processing is carried out for different types of summary descriptors (Section 2.4). For example, Utochkin and Vostrikov (2017) found no cost for dividing attention between mean size and numerosity of a set of seven to thirty-six circles with seven unique sizes.

However, pre-cue advantages were observed when two spatially intermixed sets defined by color (ten to thirty-six circles per set) were presented and observers either adjusted a test to the mean size or entered an estimate of numerosity of one set, and when they reported the mean size of one set and the numerosity of the other within the same trial. Khvostov and Utochkin (2019) next used a dual-task paradigm to examine dividing attention between mean size and numerosity or mean size and variability. Observers either adjusted one statistical summary of each set (a single test circle for the mean, or a test patch for the variance) or two summaries concurrently. In all cases, there was no evidence of a cost associated with estimating two compared to one summary descriptor of a single set. Results suggest the visual system can not only average different feature dimensions in parallel (Section 2.6.2) but can also compute different types of ensemble statistics in parallel, as long as they belong to the same set.

Overall, results suggest multiple ensemble features and statistics can be extracted from the same set in parallel. With multiple sets, a superset advantage limits capacity to compute individual summaries of the same ensemble property, and capacity is also limited for representing different ensemble features and different statistics. These findings align with individual differences discussed in Section 3.1, suggesting ensembles are encoded hierarchically over multiple stages of information processing.

To summarize what is summarized, ensemble representations are encoded for sets distributed over space and time, across a broad range of spatial and temporal properties, in multiple modalities. Much evidence suggests ensemble statistics are fundamentally encoded, and encompass rich statistical information. In addition to outlining key findings for novice readers and providing a convenient reference for experts, this section highlighted crucial methodological aspects of foundational studies. Importantly, using sparse displays may not necessitate reliance on ensemble representations. As discussed in Section 5.6, this may artificially "force" responses based on ensemble representations, even when disadvantageous to performance. While most findings have since been verified in more appropriate paradigms, it remains important for both replication and extension that original findings are henceforth referenced with applicable methodological qualifiers, and these potential confounds are not propagated in future studies. Such design constraints may well account for seemingly discrepant findings in studies discussed throughout this Element.

3 Theoretical Accounts

In addition to characterizing ensemble representations, several major theoretical aspects of how ensemble encoding is accomplished have been consistently debated. Before introducing our own account, we outline these issues and theories proposed to address them. We begin with a discussion of whether ensemble representations are encoded by an overarching, unitary mechanism. Next, we cover perhaps the most well-known debate, whether it involves qualitatively different mechanisms. We then turn to subsequent questions regarding differential contributions of individual items comprising ensembles. Finally, we discuss evidence supporting theoretical claims that ensemble encoding is automatic and obligatory. Whereas a number of theories have aimed to answer specific questions, few can address this greater collection. We propose ensemble encoding is best understood holistically in terms of RHT as the result of rapid, implicit, feedforward processing distinct from individual element perception.

3.1 Unitary versus Multiple Estimators?

Related to the discussion of whether multiple sets and descriptors can be computed in parallel (Section 2.6), there is debate regarding whether ensemble perception is accomplished by a central specialized mechanism versus a basic mechanism repeated in various cortical loci and hierarchical levels. This question is often addressed by studying individual differences, measuring correlations between performance in various tasks within the same participants. If there is substantial correlation between tasks, there is likely a common underlying process. However, interpretations of the specificity of such a common process should be treated with caution. Careful control is necessary to assure correlation is related to ensemble encoding rather than other sources of individual differences.

Haberman and colleagues (2015) measured correlations in observers' abilities to match a test stimulus to the average of a set of four stimuli across several feature dimensions. Uncorrelated performance between errors for matching the average orientation of a set of Gabors and errors in a verbal letter span memory task served as a lower bound. Highly correlated errors in matching the average orientation of high and low spatial frequency Gabors was taken as an upper bound. Similar to the moderate positive correlation between errors for matching the identity of a single face or the average identity of a set, errors were correlated for low-level features (average orientation and color of triangles, average orientation of Gabors and average color of dots, average orientations of Gabors and triangles). Errors were similarly moderately correlated between high-level features (average identity and average emotion of faces), but not correlated between high- and low-level features (average identity and average orientation of Gabors, and average emotion and color of dots). Although these patterns are taken as support that there is no "domain-general" processor for ensemble encoding, especially given similar performance for single and average identity matching, it is possible adjustments were not purely based on average representations but biased by the four individual representations (Section 5.6). This raises the question of whether findings are more indicative of the distribution of high- and low-level features for individual elements in representational space.

Chang and Gauthier (2021) similarly examined correlations between observers' performance when selecting the average of a set of four planes, birds, or cars from six test stimuli. To quantify domain-specific object recognition within each of the three categories, they also asked observers to study a display of six planes, birds, or cars (different from stimuli in the mean judgment task) and measured their accuracy when choosing which of three items was one of the six studied targets over thirty-six subsequent trials. After partialling-out variance accounted for by same-category object recognition, performance remained correlated across domains in the averaging tasks. Results were taken as support for domain-general ensemble encoding. However, observers were again asked to average displays of four objects. Furthermore, the object recognition task used test displays of six items, more likely to rely on average representation than the actual ensemble task (Section 3.4.2). Therefore, the task intended to measure object recognition may instead have measured ensemble encoding more than the ensemble task used, reiterating concerns regarding experimental design.

Even studies using stimulus displays with larger set sizes have produced conflicting results. As discussed in Section 2.6.2, Yörük and Boduroglu (2020) observed no evidence of a common mechanism based on a lack of correlation between observers' adjustment errors for matching the average length and orientation of twelve lines (cf., Chang & Gauthier, 2021 regarding potential power issues). However, Kacin and colleagues (2021) found significant correlations between length and orientation averaging using a variant of this task with modified stimuli to ensure discriminately, a larger sample size, and a 5AFC response instead of an adjustable slider. Taken together, results tentatively suggest at least some shared processing related to ensemble representations of low-level features and some shared processing for higher-level ensemble representations, but no clear commonality across feature domains.

In addition to individual differences for features, several studies asked whether various types of statistical descriptors are encoded by a common mechanism. Yang and colleagues (2018) showed observers sets of sixteen objects with different sizes (strawberries) or orientations (lollipops with tilted sticks), and asked them to adjust a probe item to match the set's mean size or orientation, or to adjust a probe set of other sixteen items to match the set's variability. There was no evidence of correlation between mean and variability estimates for size or orientation. Similarly, Utochkin and Vostrikov (2017) observed no evidence of a correlation between mean size and numerosity estimates for a single set or two distinct sets, and Khvostov and Utochkin (2019) replicated these findings for both mean-numerosity and mean-variability pairs across participants and individual trials. These findings were later challenged by Cha and colleagues (2021) who accounted for variation in single stimulus feature estimation, used a larger sample size, and found significant correlations between 2IFC judgments of the larger mean size and the greater size variability of displays of six circles. Hansmann-Roth and colleagues (2021) reported high correlations between mean color and color variability discrimination measured implicitly using a version of priming-of -popout visual search task (Section 2.4.3). After a streak of trials with a consistent color distribution of distractors, observers were asked to choose which of two test sets was more similar to the past streak. Target and foil set distributions could differ in mean color, variance, or shape. Although observers were at chance at discriminating distributions by shape, they could reliably discriminate by mean color and by color variance, with highly correlated precision between these two summaries. However, ensembles repeated several times before the test, which may have reduced the noise in otherwise uncorrelated mechanisms, retaining only common sources of representational noise.

It is also unclear when ensemble representations are constructed over the course of information processing. Joo and colleagues' (2009) findings that the accuracy of mean size judgments for displays of twelve circles (two unique sizes) decreased when some individual circles were interocularly suppressed suggest mean size computations during later stages of processing after binocular information is combined. Additional findings in Section 3.3.1 also suggest averaging after viewpoint invariant scaling. Corbett and Melcher (2014) later reported mean size adaptation using displays of fourteen differently sized circles transferred retinotopically, spatiotopically, hemispherically, and interocularly, extending mean size encoding across multiple spatial reference frames and various stages of information processing before and after inputs from the eyes converge in V1. Collectively, results suggest a single statistical processor cannot be isolated to a given stage. The ubiquity of summary statistical representations demonstrated throughout this Element further suggests this process is carried out during multiple stages of information processing.

Overall, differences in methodologies between studies do not allow for a definitive understanding of whether ensemble summaries are readout from the same kind of perceptual representations. Perhaps, new research designs are necessary to answer these questions. Nonetheless, the majority of results support a mechanism repeated at different levels of the visual hierarchy and different cerebral areas devoted to different features versus a singular mechanism at one cerebral site.

3.2 Qualitatively Different?

Perhaps the most well-known debate regarding ensemble encoding is whether this process is qualitatively different from focused attentional processing for encoding individual objects. "Does the visual system create a specific representation for a set of similar objects that is not just the sum of the representations of the individual items? (Ariely, 2001)"

3.2.1 Parallel Processing versus Sub-Sampling

Earliest reports of ensemble perception assumed a mechanism qualitatively distinct from focused attentional mechanisms. Ariely (2001) further proposed this distinct form of processing discards information about individual items, reducing the set representation to only higher-level statistical properties necessary to maintain stable global perception and identify local regions of interest. However, Myczek and Simons (2008) questioned this assumption based on simulations showing performance in multiple averaging tasks could be accounted for by subsampling strategies using focused attention instead of necessitating novel, ad hoc averaging mechanisms.

Numerous studies stemming from this debate have yielded apparently conflicting results. Rebutting subsampling accounts, Chong and colleagues (2008) noted no evidence of task-switching cost using interleaved versus blocked trials, which Myczek and Simons (2008) suggested would engage different subsampling strategies. In addition, averaging performance was significantly lower with displays of limited numbers of randomly selected elements, and performance was identical regardless of whether the largest element was presented in the larger- or smaller-average-size set. In contrast, Solomon and Morgan (2017) found equivalent performance discriminating which of two side-by-side arrays of Gabors contained a texture boundary defined by differences in mean orientation in the top and bottom of arrays with similar precision as when displays only contained arrays comprised of a single top and bottom element. Similarly, Zepp and colleagues (2021) presented items across two successive frames and found averaging performance was best modeled by subsampling two items from the second frame. Maule and Franklin (2016) reported subsampling just two items suffices to reproduce the precision of most observers' performance judging average hue. On the other hand, Alvarez and Oliva (2008) found superior performance in localizing the centroid of a set of four distractors versus the individual distractor locations in a multiple object tracking task could only be achieved if all distractors were pooled. Similarly, Semizer and Boduroglu (2021) found overestimation of mean size in high- but not low-variance displays of nine circles with similar proportions of larger-than-the-mean items between conditions such that overestimation was not based on a larger-than-the-mean subset.

As noted by Ariely (2008), perhaps the most convincing counterargument that averaging is carried out by a qualitatively different process is given by predicted performance in a membership identification task accomplished by a subsampling mechanism. If observers subsample accurate representations of a few individual items, the accuracy with which they can discriminate whether a given item was present should be a function of the number able to be selected from the set. For example, 75 percent performance is expected if observers can individually encode two of four items as in Myczek and Simons' (2008) simulations. However, no subsampling accounts to date can explain better than average mean discrimination versus chance member identification for sets of the same numbers of individual objects. Ariely (2008) further pointed out Myczek and Simons (2008) use ideal observer models that only incorporate processing errors, not fluctuations of errors over time inherent in human observations. Later explicated by Whitney and Leib (2018), as long as more than one item is subsampled, an averaging mechanism is still required.

3.2.2 Distributed versus Focused Attention

Related to sampling debate, there has been much discussion of the attentional mode involved in ensemble representation. In the attentional literature, set size manipulations are often used distinguish between limited-capacity focused attention and distributed preattentive processing (e.g., Treisman & Gelade, 1980), such that increasing the number of items in a display impedes processes that require serial but not parallel processing. Applying this logic to ensemble encoding has thus far resulted in a mixed bag of effects. However, not all studies may have necessitated relying on the average representation and therefore may not have been subject to set size effects. For example, Ariely (2001) reported observers were able to discriminate whether a test circle was larger than the mean size of the set regardless of whether sets were comprised of 4, 8, 12, or 16 circles (with four unique sizes). Chong and Treisman (2003) demonstrated observers could discriminate which of two single circles, two patches of twelve homogeneously sized circles, or two patches of twelve differently sized circles had the larger mean size. Yet, heterogeneous displays were again comprised of only four unique sizes. Similarly, Chong and Treisman (2005b) found no effect of set size when observers determined which side of displays of eight and sixteen circles had the larger average size over different distributions of only two unique sizes. When asked to discriminate whether a face was a member of a set of four to sixteen faces (with four unique emotions), Haberman and Whitney (2009) reported the frequency with which observes false-alarmed to the mean emotion was unaffected by set size. In contrast, Ji and Pourtois (2018) reported less precise averaging of facial expressions as a function of set size when participants used a slider to estimate the average emotion of a set of four to sixteen faces with unique identities but only four different emotions, but this effect disappeared with decreased variance between the unique emotions.

Yet, even studies using unique feature values yield apparently discrepant results. For example, Corbett and Oriet (2011) presented observers with RSVP streams of five to eleven circles with unique sizes and found they overwhelmingly incorrectly endorsed a test circle representing the mean size of the entire stream as being present even though they were at chance to correctly endorse tests representing sizes that were present. Allik and colleagues (2013) also observed no effect of set size when observers were presented with sets of 1, 2, 4, and 8 uniquely sized circles and indicated whether the mean size was larger than a previously presented reference, and further that mean estimates were similar regardless of whether a given size increment was distributed over all circles or applied to only one. Marchant and colleagues (2013) presented observers with sets of four to sixteen items with either two unique sizes or all unique sizes and asked them to adjust a probe to match the average size. Adjustment accuracy was unaffected by set size with only two unique sizes but decreased as a function of set size with all unique sizes.

Several studies have even reported improvements in ensemble task performance over increasing set sizes. When Robitaille and Harris (2011) presented observers with displays of two to ten uniquely sized circles and asked them to determine whether the mean size was larger than a target circle, they responded faster and more accurately as a function of increasing set size. Furthermore, when observers viewed displays of two to ten uniquely tilted lines, they exhibited opposite effects of faster and more accurate performance with increasing set size when determining whether the display mean orientation was more horizontal than a target versus slower, less accurate performance with increasing set size when determining whether the display contained the target. Brezis and colleagues (2015) presented observers with RSVP streams of 4, 8, or 16 unique two-digit numbers and asked them to estimate whether the average was larger than 50. When response time was limited, speed and accuracy increased with increasing set sizes. Using a priming-by-pop-out paradigm (Section 2.4.3), Chetverikov and colleagues (2017c) manipulated the number of 8, 14, 24, or 36 uniquely tilted lines within a streak of trials and found the entire feature distribution was learned faster with larger set sizes. Corbett and Munneke (2020) independently manipulated set size and the stability of the mean size of a display of multiple Gabors over successive trials and found observers were able to discriminate the orientation of a target singleton faster purely as a function of mean size stability whereas search times slowed only as a function of increasing set size. This pattern suggests increasing set size does not affect the benefits of ensemble stability on visual search discussed further in Section 5.4.

To account for some of these discrepancies, Utochkin and Tiurina (2014) proposed set size effects may be modulated by the range of feature values. They first replicated Marchant and colleagues (2013) findings of set size effects when observers discriminated which of four subsequently presented test dots matched the average size of sets of 4, 8, or 16 items comprised of either two unique sizes or with all unique sizes. Similar to findings by Ji and Pourtois (2018), set size effects disappeared when variance between displays with all unique items and only two unique sizes was controlled. Maule and Franklin (2015) also reported no set size effects when variance was controlled. Participants were presented with displays of four to sixteen circles and determined which of two test circles represented the average hue. Importantly, results described so far used many different methods and features, making it difficult to offer any definitive answers regarding the overarching effects of set size. Future studies considering these issues will hopefully clarify the nature of set size effects in ensemble encoding.

Importantly, detrimental effects of set size on averaging should not be directly interpreted as evidence for low-capacity processing and facilitating or absent effects should likewise not be directly interpreted as evidence for high-capacity processing. Capacity can also be assessed by asking how many individual objects are effectively averaged. Using equivalent noise analysis, internal noise and capacity can be estimated as a function of set size by measuring performance at different levels of stimulus uncertainty. Each individual item is encoded with a certain amount of early sensory noise that may change with set size, then a subset is efficiently sampled for averaging (Figure 3a, b). Dakin (2001) first used equivalent noise analysis to show the effective sample size for orientation averaging is approximately equal to the square root of the set size. Dakin and colleagues (2005) obtained similar estimates for average direction of motion, regardless of the density of individual elements or the overall area they occupied. Although similar estimates were obtained for averaging, even more precise representations were observed for set orientation (Solomon, 2010) and size (Solomon et al., 2011) variance. Im and Halberda (2013) obtained estimates for size averaging of up to twenty-three elements suggesting internal noise was less than individual element noise. In theory, the square-root growth of the sample size in proportion to set size is sufficient to account for detrimental set size effects despite variability across different feature dimensions (Figure 3c).

Allik and colleagues (2013) suggested a Noise-and-Selection model of ensemble perception, predicated on the assumptions that not all items are included in the mean computation, and each item that is included carries some degree of noise independent of set size. In this model, an individual's internal noise level can be derived from their precision determining single element size. However, it is important to note performance in discriminating a test circle from the mean is not subject to the same illusory conjunctions as recalling the size of an individual circle in a specific location (e.g., Treisman & Gelade, 1980). In any case, it is not immediately apparent how such subsampling models reconcile with findings that performance stays constant or even improves with larger set sizes.

An alternative way of modeling set size effects is to sample all items to some degree. Such a model proposed by Baek and Chong (2020a) predicts when many noisy and uncorrelated measurements are averaged, individual measurement errors of non-systematically varying magnitudes and directions average out to eliminate this error in the overall pooled estimate, such that average representations become more precise than individual measurements. This noise cancellation benefits from increasing individual measurements with uncorrelated errors (Figure 3d, e). However, if early encoding noise also increases with set size (e.g., Dakin, 2001), this can counteract noise cancellation (Figure 3f). Framing ensemble averaging as a balance between early individual element encoding noise and noise cancellation allows for a unitary account of set size effects without the need to imply different sampling capacities (Figure 3g). If early noise grows rapidly with set size, noise cancellation is insufficient to compensate and there is a detrimental effect of set size. If early noise grows slower, noise cancellation can compensate with invariance or even facilitation of averaging.

Although extreme versions of subsampling theory suggest ensemble encoding can be completely explained within the scope of focused attention, Baek and Chong's (2020a) distributed attention model better predicts several aspects of typical averaging performance, such as saturation for smaller set size due to attention being spread more completely over fewer items, increased performance due to greater noise cancellation at larger set sizes, and asymptotic

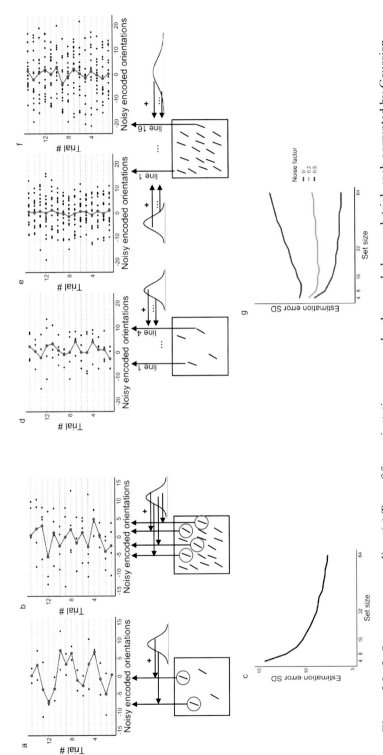

Figure 3 Left: Square root sampling. (a) Two of four orientations are randomly sampled on each trial, each corrupted by Gaussian noise (black dots), and the mean is calculated (red dots; red line tracks trial-to-trial sample average) (b) Four of sixteen orientations are

Caption for Figure 3 (cont.)

randomly sampled with the same amount of Gaussian noise. (c) The standard deviation of sample averages around the set mean shrinks with set size. Right: Exhaustive averaging. (d) All four items are sampled and corrupted by Gaussian noise with $\sigma = 4$.

(e) If noise remains constant over set size, all items sixteen are sampled with the same amount of noise ($\sigma = 4$). (f) If noise grows with set size, all sixteen elements are sampled with increased noise ($\sigma = 8$). (g) Precision improves as a function of set size if noise does not change (noise factor = 0); precision remains approximately the same if noise grows by 0.2 per item (noise factor = 0.2); and precision drops with set size if noise grows faster than noise cancellation (noise factor = 0.5).

performance for increasingly large set sizes due to late internal noise. The spread of attention over items can be thought of as a continuum from extremely focused local attention dedicated to processing items at maximum resolution, to broadly distributed global attention over multiple items at cost to resolution. Whereas focused attention is associated with tasks requiring object individuation, ensemble perception is more associated with distributed processing without requiring explicit knowledge of individual objects (e.g., Treisman, 2006). Indeed, there is evidence performance on ensemble tasks benefits from shifting to a more distributed processing mode. Most notably, Chong and Treisman (2005a) found more accurate performance in a size averaging task when it was combined with an easy visual search for a closed circle among open circles requiring parallel, distributed attention, compared to a difficult search for an open circle among closed circles requiring serially focused attention to individual items.

3.2.3 Is Attention Necessary?

In addition to the question of whether distributed attentional mechanisms underlie ensemble encoding, it remains unclear whether attention is necessary at all. This question is typically addressed using various manipulations to divert or attenuate attention and measure an unattended ensemble's influence on performance, measuring performance in an ensemble task under increased processing loads, or in patient populations with atypical attentional processing.

Multiple studies report intact ensemble encoding when attention is selectively directed away from the to-be-encoded set. Alvarez and Oliva (2008, 2009; Section 2.1.6) used an attention-demanding multiple object tracking task requiring observers to constantly monitor one set of four independently moving objects while ignoring a second set of moving objects or ignoring a constantly changing background consisting of differently oriented Gabors. Even when attention was withdrawn and observers could not report the individual locations of elements, they were still able to accurately indicate the centroid location of all the elements in both the unattended and attended sets and detect global changes in the average orientation of the background, suggesting ensemble but not individual information is relatively preserved under conditions of diverted attention. Chen and Zhou (2018) later reported ensemble summaries of groups of both tracked and untracked faces unintentionally affected item recognition, although tracked face subsets exerted a stronger influence.

Bronfman and colleagues (2014) tested whether observers extracted an impression of color variability from multiple items outside an attended subset. Observers viewed arrays of color letters and were asked to remember all the letters from a particular row. Apart from the main letter recall task, observers could report how diverse the colors of letters in the attended and unattended rows were with similar accuracy. Extending these results, Ward and colleagues (2016) modulated individual letter colors while holding variance constant and found judgments remained accurate despite change blindness for individual colors. However, Jackson-Nielsen and colleagues (2017) implicitly tested color diversity judgments using a task where observers had to recall all letters in a pre-cued row, then were unexpectedly asked which of three probes (one matching the ensemble color or size variance, one not matching, and one with the same color or size variance as the nonmatching but with upside-down letters) was most similar to or had the same variance as the previous display. Many observers showed inattentional blindness, incorrectly selecting nonmatching probes, suggesting attention was necessary for a conscious impression of the ensemble. To reconcile with earlier findings, the authors proposed at least *some* attention was needed for conscious ensemble perception. However, an alternative explanation for this null effect is that it would be impractical for participants to retain a conscious perception of background information that is irrelevant to the main attention-demanding letter recall task but it can nonetheless influence perception (e.g., Moore & Egeth, 1997).

Several studies have reported ensembles encoding even when processing resources are engaged in another attention-demanding task. Dakin et al. (2009) asked observers to report the orientation of an oddball white T in a sequence of black T's at fixation either before (low load) or after (high load) estimating whether the overall tilt of a set of Gabors was clockwise or counterclockwise. Overall, results suggested ensembles are extracted with decreased precision under high central attentional load. However, Epstein and Emmanouil (2017) found no evidence for an effect of high working memory load on average discrimination. Observers' discriminations of which of two patches of twelve circles each set (with four unique sizes) had the larger average size were unaffected by having to perform a low (displays of two-colored squares) or high (displays of four-colored squares) object memory task to determine whether the color of a square had changed over two successive displays or a low (displays of two white squares) or high (displays of four white squares) spatial memory task determining whether the location of a square changed. Bauer (2017) found evidence that increasing working memory load by increasing the length of a to-be-remembered string of four to seven digits actually increased the precision with which observers discriminated whether a probe line was longer than the average line length.

In contrast, several studies using paradigms known to deplete attention and prevent conscious awareness have found explicit effects of ensemble encoding.

Joo and colleagues (2009) demonstrated mean size is represented even when focused attentional resources are depleted using an attentional blink paradigm (Raymond et al., 1992) in which observers were asked to identify two targets in RSVP streams of single items. Observers exhibited typical patterns of performance and were less able to detect the second target (T2) when it was presented in close temporal succession to the first target (T1), which presumably was still engaging central attentional resources. When T2 displays were composed of two displays of sixteen circles (different proportions of two unique sizes), accuracy to discriminate which side of T2 had the larger average size remained similar across lags, suggesting even though individual items were blinked from conscious perception, they were nonetheless included in the average.

Choo and Franconeri (2010) presented observers with displays of eight circles and asked them to judge whether a test circle was larger than the average. When two of the circles were surrounded by a four-dot mask to prevent them from reaching conscious awareness (object substitution masking), observers still included these circles in their average discriminations. However, Jacoby and colleagues (2013) reported this ability to average masked circles disappeared when they were restricted to opposite sides of the display to prevent spatial overlap that may have otherwise captured attention.

Also using an attentional blink paradigm, Corbett and Oriet (2011) implicitly tested ensemble encoding by measuring observers' abilities to identify an outlier circle (T2) noticeably larger or smaller than nine other uniquely sized circles in RSVP streams of circles immediately followed by RSVP streams of shapes in which observers had to discriminate a target shape (T1). When presented with a test circle after the sequence, observers incorrectly selected the mean of the entire sequence as being present over an outlier that was present. Although most pronounced at shorter lags when central attentional resources were still engaged in processing T1, observers still false-alarmed to the mean at longer lags, but were able to correctly discriminate the outlier from a foil that was neither the mean nor present. A further study by McNair and colleagues (2017) using a set of four face stimuli reported similar findings for average emotion and gender.

Studies of patient populations with absent or compromised attentional mechanisms have demonstrated ensemble representations survive when individual objects comprising ensembles cannot be consciously perceived. For example, unilateral spatial neglect (USN) is a common neurological disorder usually caused by right hemisphere damage, characterized by a failure to attend stimuli on the contralesional side (e.g., Driver & Vuilleumier, 2001). Extinction is commonly observed in USN, where patients disregard a contralesional stimulus with simultaneous bilateral stimulation, although the same stimulus may be detected when presented in isolation (e.g., de Haan, Karnath, & Driver, 2012).

Yamanashi Leib and colleagues (2012) reported averaging despite extinction in four patients with mild chronic left-side neglect. After presentation of a target circle, the task was to search for a circle of the same size presented in a cloud of various-sized circles all on one side of the display and triangle distractors on the other side. The average hit rate was 50 percent on the left, compared with 70 percent on the right, confirming extinction. Most interestingly, when the target was absent, the false-alarm rate was greater when the mean circle was the same size as the target, but only for left-side clouds. Taken with the finding that left-side distractor triangle size also affected right-side search, results suggest patients implicitly computed mean size in the neglected field.

Pavlovskaya, Hochstein and colleagues (2015) also studied ensemble perception in USN patients, using three different tasks. In all cases, a reference circle appeared at fixation, then a blank screen, followed by a unilateral or bilateral array of nonoverlapping circles, with an average size larger or smaller than the reference. Observers judged whether the average size of the array was larger than the reference. With unilateral presentation, patients and controls performed above 75 percent correct for either side, but patient performance was significantly reduced for left- versus right-side presentation, whereas controls showed similar performance for the two sides. Patients' performance deficits were stronger when averaging left-side elements in cases of extinction with items simultaneously presented on the right. Critically, with bilateral arrays, the two sides had different sizes to allow for measurement of whether only one or both sides were included in the average. Patients showed deficient performance in conditions where the left side of the array had a larger difference from the reference. Nevertheless, their performance was significantly worse for the right-side condition compared with the both-sides condition (which differ only in left-side average), indicating "neglected" left-side circles did contribute to the average. Results provide converging evidence USN impairment is limited to focused attention mechanisms, and distributed attention mechanisms largely spared in USN are involved in ensemble encoding (Section 3.2.2).

Further evidence that ensemble statistics can be encoded with reduced or no focused attention in USN is given by findings that repeating the global mean size while randomly varying the sizes of individual Gabors improved search for an orientation singleton target (Lanzoni et al., 2014), similar to patterns of performance in neurotypical controls and in previous studies with neurotypical observers (Section 5.4). The involvement of distributed versus focused attention in ensemble encoding is also supported by findings that patients with simultanagnosia, who can reliably attend to only a single item, nonetheless make accurate estimates of mean color and size for displays of multiple circles (Demeyere et al., 2008), and patients with prosopagnosia, who have difficulty recognizing faces, nevertheless accurately estimate the average identity and emotion of crowds (Yamanashi-Leib et al., 2012). Collectively, reports of intact ensemble encoding in patients with atypical focused attentional processing provide converging evidence ensemble perception depends on a global mechanism rather than on focused attention and subsampling.

In contrast to neglect patients, autistic individuals show enhanced local processing of features and fine detail (e.g., Happé & Frith, 2006). So far, studies of ensemble encoding in individuals with Autism Spectrum Disorder (ASD) have returned seemingly discrepant results. Corbett and colleagues (2016) found above-chance accuracy in recalling the mean size of a set of circles despite poor accuracy in recalling individual circle sizes (membership task), in line with superior mean versus member performance in the general population. Furthermore, ASD judgments of single circle size were biased by mean size adaptation, suggesting averaging was automatic and implicit. Karaminis and colleagues (2017) also found no evidence of differences between autistic and neurotypical children's precision in ensemble and baseline emotion discrimination, and face identification. This collection of findings further underscores the fundamental nature of ensemble encoding.

However, additional studies have found differences in ensemble perception in ASD. Maule and colleagues (2016) presented sets of four to sixteen colored discs and asked participants whether a single item was present, or which of two items matched the mean color. Autistic adults were slightly more sensitive in detecting membership but performed similarly to controls in the mean task. However, with four element sets, autistic participants needed a greater difference between tests than controls in the mean task. Rhodes and colleagues (2015) also found children with autism correctly identified members of sets of four faces more frequently, and were less prone to identify missing mean faces as having been present. Lowe and colleagues (2018) presented neurotypical participants with differing sensitivities to sensory input (assuming higher sensitivity in ASD) with an array of nine circles comprised of three circles in three colors, and asked them to remember the sizes of circles in two of the colors and ignore circles in the third color. When recalling the size of a single circle, participants demonstrated bias toward the mean size of the probed color as an inverse function of sensory sensitivity. Importantly, these discrepancies between ASD and neurotypical averaging generally result with displays of relatively small set sizes, even more likely to be encoded using focused attention by individuals with ASD. As discussed further in Section 5.6, these findings may actually be the result of superior individual object versus inferior ensemble representation in ASD.

Overall, results converge in favor of qualitatively different processes underlying ensemble versus individual item encoding. Although some distributed attention may be necessary for conscious perception, ensemble representations nonetheless implicitly affect behavior and survive even when focused attentional resources are compromised.

3.3 Contributions of Individual Elements

In addition to the question of whether ensemble encoding is accomplished by qualitatively different mechanisms, it is unclear how individual elements contribute to ensemble representations. We first review findings regarding whether ensemble representations contain information about individual elements. Next, we discuss possible visual field differences in individual item contributions and reports ensemble representations can be distorted by salient members but remain robust with respect to obvious outliers. Finally, we review converging evidence that ensemble statistics are computed directly, not inferred from individual components.

3.3.1 Do Ensemble Representations Contain Any Individuated Information?

Multiple studies report ensemble perception is possible even when detailed information necessary to perceive individual elements is unavailable due to crowding. Parkes and colleagues (2001) first demonstrated observers could not discriminate the orientation of a grating surrounded by a ring of similar gratings presented peripherally, but the orientation of this grating was nonetheless included in calculations of average orientation. Fischer and Whitney (2011) obtained similar results for average emotion of crowded sets of faces. Dakin and colleagues (2009) independently manipulated crowding within a set of differently oriented Gabors and attention using a demanding central task to report the orientation of an oddball white T embedded in a sequence of black T's either before (low load) or after (high load) estimating whether the overall tilt of the Gabors was clockwise or counterclockwise. Crowding and attention exhibited independent influences on averaging performance, such that crowding decreased item precision, whereas attentional load modulated averaging efficiency.

Evidence of context-based rescaling suggests ensemble encoding operates over individuated objects. Given the retinal size of an object changes dramatically as a function of viewing distance but perceived size remains constant until distance information is available (Holway & Boring, 1941), the ability to rescale retinal image properties into a context-invariant representation is necessary to maintain perceptual constancy. Tiurina and Utochkin (2019) used stereoscopic displays to present observers with sets of circles perceived at various apparent distances. When asked to adjust the size of a probe to match the average, observers exaggerated the mean size of objects presented at farther apparent distances. Observers were also shown objects of different retinal sizes at four different apparent distances either positively correlated (the bigger the size, the farther the distance) or negatively correlated. The positive correlation amplified the apparent contrast between smallest and largest items (e.g., largest items far away appeared even larger) and negative correlations attenuated this contrast. Observers demonstrated typical range effects (Section 2.4.2), with decreased precision for positive-correlation displays. Given the distributions of retinal sizes and depth planes were identical in both conditions, results suggest size-distance rescaling involved in averaging cannot simply be explained by the computation of average 2D size rescaled by average distance but instead preceded by rescaling of individual item sizes as a function of their apparent distances. Markov and Tiurina (2021) later extended these results to variance perception.

Im and Chong (2009) used stimuli presented in different configurations to further demonstrate context-based rescaling in size averaging. Observers compared the mean sizes of two sets of central circles (on opposite sides of fixation), surrounded by either smaller or larger circles. Although instructed to only compare the mean sizes of the central sets, judgments were biased as an inverse function of the size of the surrounding circles (i.e., Ebbinghaus Illusion). These findings strongly suggest ensemble summaries are subject to configural and contextual interactions during mid- to high-level stages of representation, involving at least some information about individual objects. Haberman and Suresh (2021) demonstrated size–distance rescaling in average size perception is also induced by pictorial depth cues. Findings that averaging precision is modulated by size–distance correlation suggest rescaling involves at least some knowledge of how individual sizes and distances are bound. Yamanashi Leib and colleagues (2014) observed viewpoint invariance in face identity averaging such that observers were fairly accurate in adjusting a forward-facing test to match the mean identity of a set of 1, 2, 4, or 18 (six unique faces) sequentially presented faces regardless of whether the set was all oriented 22.5° leftwards or each face was randomly presented at one of three orientations (90° leftwards, 22.5° leftwards, and 22.5° rightwards). Taken together, findings collectively suggest ensemble representations involve at least some information about distinct elements, but do not necessarily require individual object encoding.

3.3.2 Location Bias

The distinction between foveal and peripheral vision reflects qualitative and quantitative differences in neuroanatomy and visual experience. Foveal vision is associated with fine resolution well-tuned for identifying individual objects and details. Peripheral vision is more broadly tuned to coarser information rendering it more sensitive to transient objects and events. Given proposals that ensembles can be represented without encoding individual elements, foveal vision should not play a special role in summary representation. Along these lines, Chong and colleagues (2008) found no evidence of differences in size averaging for items spread across the entire visual field compared to items clustered around fixation. Wolfe and colleagues (2015) came to a similar conclusion in a series of eye-tracking experiments in which observers estimated the average emotion of a set of faces. Averaging during gaze-contingent occlusion of foveal stimuli was similar to performance in a baseline no-occlusion condition, suggesting ensemble representations were accomplished without foveal input. However, when Ji and colleagues (2014) varied the ratio of happy and sad faces in foveal and peripheral regions, items near fixation had a larger influence on perceived average emotion. Findings indicate ensemble statistics can be efficiently encoded for peripheral information where details are less visible and individuation can be complicated by crowding, yet foveal information may contribute uniquely when central and peripheral items are simultaneously available. Collectively, results suggest ensemble perception can be based both on coarse, "texture-like" information and fine information associated with detailed individual object perception in line with roles of focused and distributed attention discussed in Section 3.2.2.

Spatial asymmetry in the retinotopic representation of the visual field has also been identified in ensemble perception. Li and Yeh (2017) reported a left-side bias in a size-averaging task using differently sized dots presented on both sides of fixation. The mean size of one-half of the display was always larger. When the larger mean size was on the left versus right side, observers tended to overestimate the whole set mean more. This bias was modulated by spatial attention such that when a spatial cue shifted attention to the left, averages were even more biased toward the mean size on the left, and this bias was attenuated or abolished when attention shifted to the right. Similarly, Pascucci and colleagues (2021) used a spatially weighted average model to demonstrate left-side bias in size averaging for displays of dots presented at different degrees of foveal dispersion, displays with stimuli exclusively presented to one visual field, and when observers were pre-cued to attend one side of bilateral displays. Both studies outline various possible mechanisms, such as the overall right-hemisphere advantage in processing holistic information, left-to-right reading-scanning habits, and the relationship to left-side asymmetry in the deployment of attention.

3.3.3 Amplification Bias

The debate between parallel exhaustive processing and limited-capacity sub-sampling has generally been presented as two opposite views of the mechanisms underlying ensemble computation. The resolution of this apparent controversy may lie in a hybrid model, whereby global ensemble statistics are biased by local array elements when these are salient and attended. Such a hybrid model was originally suggested by De Fockert and Marchant (2008) after observing attention to a single large/small set element skews perception of average size similar to the manner in which larger versus smaller feature values usually attract attention more efficiently (Treisman & Gormican, 1988). A recent study by Goldenberg and colleagues (2021) demonstrated similar amplification of crowd emotion driven by attentional bias to emotional faces. Choi and Chong (2020) compared the effects of selective attention increasing the perceived size versus the weighted contribution of an item on mean size computations by pre-cueing and post-cueing one of eight circular gratings in a radial array and tasking observers to adjust a test to the set's mean size and discriminate the clockwise or counterclockwise orientation of the cued grating. Pre-cued mean size adjustments were biased by both perceptual enlargement and overall greater weighting of the cued grating, suggesting mean size representations can be modulated by altering the appearance of pre-cued items in addition to effects of weighted averaging observed in the post-cue condition. Iakovlev and Utochkin (2021) also reported size amplification bias in variability perception, implying limited-capacity attentional sampling of salient items.

A hybrid model is further supported by results from Dodgson and Raymond's (2020) study in which they trained observers to attribute higher value to elements of a certain color and found mean size judgments were biased toward sizes of elements presented in that color. This bias disappeared with masked presentations. Results suggest only rapidly acquired prioritized ensemble statistics survive when processing time is limited, but salient elements are also combined into averages with longer processing time. Munneke and colleagues (2022) recently reported a similar bias of average size representations toward larger sizes presented in colors previously associated with high rewards. Saliency-based amplification bias in average flicker frequency (Section 2.1.13) and serial order effects on averaging induced by temporally salient objects (Section 2.3.2) have also been previously reported.

3.3.4 Outlier Discount

On the "flip-side," several studies have demonstrated outlying feature values that would otherwise introduce amplification bias do not affect ensemble representation. For example, Haberman and Whitney (2010) had observers adjust the mean emotion of a set of twelve faces in which ten faces were drawn from a narrow range around the mean and two dramatically deviated from that range. Adjustments were more tightly concentrated around the local mean of ten faces than the global mean of all twelve. When a contour of highly similar orientations was embedded within a larger display of differently tilted Gabors, observers similarly did not include this outlier contour in average orientation estimations (Cha & Chong, 2018). Along these lines, Utochkin and Tiurina (2014) reported averaging can occur for all items in parallel, but this computation is hampered when some items differ too much.

De Gardelle and Summerfield (2011) referred to the mechanism that protects ensemble representations from biasing effects of items with no relation to the group as *robust averaging*. They reported judgments of whether the average color of a set of eight circles was more red or blue or whether the average shape was more circular or square were best approximated by a model basing perceptual decisions mainly on inlying colors/shapes, deweighting, or discounting outlying values in heterogeneous displays. Based on findings that observers who weighted outliers less in their estimates of whether the mean orientation of a radial array of eight Gabors was more tilted than the orientation of a central reference, Li and colleagues' (2017) simulations of robust averaging resulted in enhanced performance, optimizing averaging in the presence of late noise that corrupts average estimates. This enhancement is not predicted by an ideal observer model that perfectly incorporates individual elements. Therefore, given noisy input and integration processes underlying ensemble representation, robust averaging is a clear strategy to optimize information integration.

Somewhat opposite to Dodgson and Raymond's (2020) findings, Epstein and colleagues (2020) found mean adjustments were skewed toward an outlier when the time between a target ensemble and mask was short. However, this bias disappeared gradually as the interval became longer, suggesting outlier discount is a relatively slow, iterative process. In a subsequent electroencephalography (EEG) study, Epstein and Emmanouil (2021) presented observers with sets of tilted lines with fixed mean orientations and asked them to detect when an "oddball" set with a different mean orientation or with the same mean but some outlier orientations occurred. The resultant P3b, an event-related potential related to visual awareness, had a shorter latency when the oddball set had a different mean versus when it included outliers but kept the same mean, suggesting ensemble information was processed earlier than outlier information. Taken together, findings imply dealing with outliers involves both feedforward and feedback processing. In Section 5.3.2, we elaborate further on how ensemble encoding may serve as a mechanism for detecting salient outliers not included in summary representations.

3.3.5 Mathematical Relation

Considering the contributions of individual elements ultimately raises the question of whether ensemble statistics are computed in accordance with mathematical statistics such as the arithmetic mean (Figure 4a) or directly without the need for intermediate representation of individual elements (Figure 4b).

One approach to understanding the nature of computations underlying ensemble summary statistics is to gauge the degree to which they can be predicted as a function of their individual parts. Along these lines, multiple studies discussed in Section 2 demonstrated the same Stevens's Power Law relationship for physical and perceived average stimulus properties as between physical and perceived individual properties of length, tilt, and brightness of individual items. Similarly, perceived average animacy (Yamanashi Leib et al., 2016) and economic value (Yamanashi Leib et al., 2020) can be predicted based on individual estimates for ensemble members.

Although ensemble and individual item statistics exhibit similar relationships between physical and perceived magnitudes, this does not necessarily mean

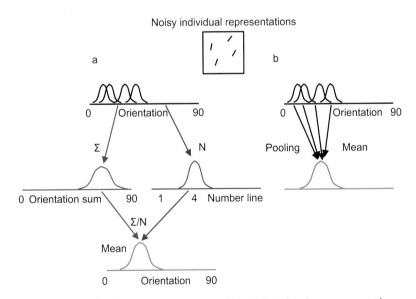

Figure 4 (a), *Arithmetic averaging:* First, individual noisy representations produce two separate summaries: sum and quantity. Then, the sum is divided by quantity. (b) *Direct averaging:* Individual signals are immediately pooled, representing the mean without necessitating intermediary representations.

ensemble statistics are inferred in a secondary manner. Lee and colleagues (2016) tested for such relationships between numerosity, mean size, and total area, which each can be expressed as a function of the other two. Observers viewed displays of 10, 20, or 40 dots presented in one of three possible mean sizes in 16 percent increments, and one of three possible densities in 16 percent increments, then judged whether the magnitude of a test stimulus (a single dot for area or the sum of all sizes, a patch of homogeneous dots for numerosity, and a single circle for mean size) was greater than the previous display. Resultant psychometric functions had steeper slopes for mean size versus numerosity and area discriminations, suggesting mean size was discriminated more precisely. Furthermore, area discrimination was well predicted by mean size and numerosity discrimination, but neither numerosity nor mean size discrimination was well predicted by the discrimination of remaining two properties. Raidvee and colleagues (2020) similarly reported more precise mean size versus total size discrimination. Together, results suggest mean size and numerosity are directly represented, not inferred from more primary statistics.

Allik and colleagues (2013) directly examined whether perceived mean size was computed as a function of the associative law of arithmetics. They presented observers with a reference circle for 500 ms followed by a display of 1, 2, 4, or 8 circles for 200 ms or 1,000 ms, and asked them to judge whether the mean size of the circles was larger than the reference. Across all set sizes, mean estimates were similar regardless of whether a given size increment was distributed over all circles or applied to only one display element. Taken with findings that observers were comparatively poor at judging the sizes of one circle at a given location (Allik et al., 2014), they concluded mean perception is indeed based on direct averaging versus inference from individual items.

Regardless of how individual objects are encoded, findings collectively suggest mean features of sets can be computed directly, and point to computational mechanisms for ensemble statistics distinct from the computation of the arithmetic mean.

It seems ensemble representations are linked to at least some information about distinct elements, but not necessarily predicated on individual item encoding. Whereas ensemble representations can be modulated by factors such as the ability of fine- versus coarse grained-information, and salient objects can skew set estimates, much evidence suggests encoding remains robust, allowing for the exclusion or segmentation of items too different from the collective. Evidence also suggests the manner in which ensembles are encoded is computationally distinct from calculating the arithmetic mean of individual elements, implying summary representations retain some link to but are not directly derived from individual item representations.

3.4 Obligatory?

Although numerous results suggest the process involved in ensemble encoding is engaged automatically, most studies explicitly ask observers to calculate the average, often in situations where individual representations could also be accessed. Dubé and Sekuler (2015) comprehensively reviewed findings that single object representations are indeed averaged regardless of explicit instruction, suggesting obligatory ensemble representation. Negative AAEs (Section 2.5) also suggest ensemble properties are implicitly encoded even if this prevents veridical object perception. Here we consider further evidence that set statistics are encoded incidentally, perhaps even in an obligatory manner.

3.4.1 Incidental Representation

Corbett and Oriet (2011) first reported when observers viewed RSVP streams of five to eleven circles (Figure 5a), their discriminations of whether a circle presented before the stream represented a member or the mean size of the stream were similarly accurate (mean judgment; Figure 5b). However, they were even more accurate in discriminating whether a circle presented after the stream represented its mean size, but could not discriminate whether the circle was a member of the stream (member identification; Figure 5b), even when explicitly asked to determine whether it was the largest circle. These findings strongly suggest the mean was automatically encoded regardless of whether

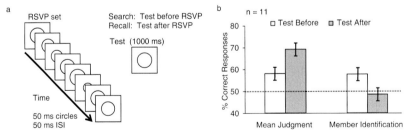

Figure 5 (a) Observers were presented with RSVP sequences of circles and a test either before or after the sequence. In the mean judgment task, they determined whether the test represented the sequence mean size. In the member identification task, they determined whether the test was a member of the sequence. (b) When the test was presented before the sequence, observers were able to determine whether it was the mean or a member with similar accuracy. However, when the test was presented after the sequence, they were most accurate in the mean judgment but near chance at member identification.
Source: Adapted from Corbett and Oriet, 2011

observers were explicitly instructed to search for or implicitly asked to recall it, and despite their inability to implicitly recall individual sizes.

Oriet and Hozempa (2016) demonstrated statistical representations of sets are incidentally constructed and can be consciously reported even when participants had no instruction or apparent intention to do so. Participants completed one of three different tasks evaluating an irrelevant dimension of displays of circles (whether there were more than fifteen circles present, whether there were two of the same color circle present, or passive viewing). Afterward, they were presented with a test and instructed to adjust it to the mean, smallest, then largest circle of the entire set of 4,200 circles. Although never previously asked anything about the sizes of the circles, they could accurately reproduce the mean, upper and lower bounds, and could even adjust a bar graph to represent the distribution.

3.4.2 False Alarms to the Mean

In line with incidental encoding, there is striking evidence dating as far back as Hollingworth (1910) (Section 1.1) that observers automatically and implicitly represent task-irrelevant mean properties of sets to the extent that they "false alarm," mistakenly remembering items representing the mean when no such items were actually presented.

In Corbett and Oriet's (2011) study, regardless of whether observers searched an RVSP sequence for a target or recalled whether it was present in the sequence, they made more false alarms, incorrectly endorsing a circle as representing the mean as being present as a linear function of how similar it was to the mean. Using similar methods, Khayat and Hochstein (2018) presented observers with RSVP displays (100 ms display and 100 ms ISI) of twelve objects with different sizes, orientations, or brightness levels, then asked them to discriminate which of two tests was a member of the set. Observers preferentially selected tests near or at the mean regardless of whether the test was actually present in the set and correctly rejected test stimuli outside the set range, suggesting they automatically encoded both the mean and range of the set even though there was no explicit instruction to do so, this was task-irrelevant, and lead to incorrect performance. These mean and range effects extended to familiar (Figure 6; Khayat & Hochstein, 2019) and novel (amoebas; Khayat et al., 2021) object categories, further suggesting the average is akin to the prototypical or canonical value of a bounded-range set.

Numerous additional studies have reported false alarms to the mean in tasks probing individual object identification. Although not an exhaustive list, many have already been described throughout this Element, such as for hue by Maule and colleagues (2014), emotional expression (Haberman & Whitney, 2009),

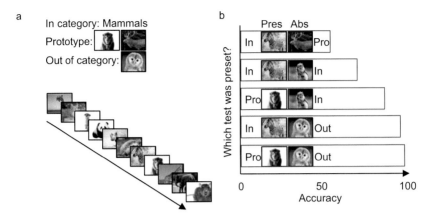

Figure 6 (a) Observers were presented with RSVP sequences of familiar objects drawn from a given category (e.g., mammals). (b) When deciding which of two tests was present in the sequence, observers made more false alarms, incorrectly choosing a prototypical object over an item that was present and within the category (PresIn vs. AbsPro). A combination of mean and range effects is further illustrated over the increasing pattern of accurate responses for present versus absent in-category tests (PresIn vs. AbsIn), present prototypical tests versus absent in-category tests (PresPro vs. AbsIn), present in-category tests versus absent out-of-category tests (PresIn vs. AbsOut), and present prototypical tests versus absent out-of-category tests (PresPro vs. AbsOut).
Source: Adapted from Khayat and Hochstein, 2019

unfamiliar (de Fockert & Wolfenstein, 2009), and familiar faces (Neumann et al., 2013). This implicit bias for the mean was found to persist in neglect patients searching for a target on the left side of displays (Yamanashi Leib et al., 2012), and was noted to be greater for collectivistic cultures (Peng et al., 2020). Sama and colleagues' (2021) recent findings that items within range of the set but not actually present in the set were misidentified as present to the same extent as items that were correctly identified as present further suggest individual items are not only inferred relative to their relations to the mean but also with reference to the set's range.

Studies demonstrating implicit representation of set properties even when there is neither instruction to do so nor task-relevance strongly support the idea that ensemble encoding happens incidentally, implicitly, and automatically. Further, findings that observers falsely believe the average or prototype of a set was presented suggest this sort of encoding may be unavoidable even if it compromises performance. However, this does not necessarily mean ensemble information is always more influential over individual item representations.

Along these lines, in Section 5.6, we elaborate on the possibility that ensemble encoding and individual item representation are utilized in a perceptually intelligent manner balancing demands for capacity and fidelity.

A complete understanding of ensemble encoding is challenged to account for this collection of theoretical questions. Results so far favor a hierarchically distributed network, qualitatively distinct from more well-understood focused-attentional processing. Although specific contributions of individual items seem to vary circumstantially and set representations are not a direct product of constituent items, there is at least some link between individual and ensemble representations. Finally, it seems ensemble encoding is ubiquitous and even obligatory, yet it is unclear under what conditions summary representations are accessed or directly influential in perceptual processing. Overall, ensemble encoding is best understood in terms of rapid, automatic global attention mechanisms retaining information at multiple levels of abstraction without requiring individual element perception.

3.5. RHT

Theoretical accounts discussed so far have all been targeted to explain a specific set of issues. As introduced in Section 1.2, we propose ensemble encoding is best understood within the framework of the RHT (Hochstein & Ahissar, 2002). Importantly, we are not arguing against other theoretical accounts discussed, but in favor of RHT as a broad, all-encompassing account. Importantly, most theoretical explanations start with the assumption information is processed and accessed in a feedforward, hierarchical manner, with low-level properties represented early on, and higher-order properties, objects, and categories abstracted over later stages of processing. In contrast, RHT (Figure 7) proposes explicit perception starts at these later, higher-level stages of processing, with hierarchical feedforward processing occurring implicitly. Explicit perception of lower-level properties requiring focused attention is accomplished by reversing this hierarchy to access representations implicitly constructed at earlier stages. Setting the access point of conscious perception at the top of the hierarchy allows for a straightforward explanation of "seeing the forest before the trees," or rapid summary perception.

In the context of RHT, ensemble processing collects low-cortical-level information into higher-level, large receptive field representations, disregarding details to represent object types and categories. Rapid conscious perception reflects this higher-level categorical representation, maintained as a condensed summary in working memory, immediately available to conscious perception, and therefore reportable. However, lower-level detailed information from

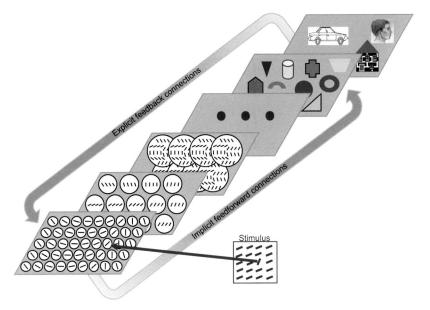

Figure 7 Classical Hierarchy and Reverse Hierarchy Theory. Classically, the visual system was seen as a hierarchy such that low-level area neurons receive visual input and represent simple features, their outputs are integrated over successive cortical levels, and gradually generalized over spatial parameters to ultimately represent global features and categories. Reverse hierarchy theory instead proposes this forward hierarchy acts implicitly, with explicit perception beginning at high-level cortex, representing the gist of the scene on the basis of a first-order approximate integration of low-level input. Later, explicit perception returns to lower areas via feedback connections to integrate detailed information into conscious "vision-with-scrutiny."
Source: Adapted from Hochstein and Ahissar, 2002

which it is built is no longer retained and must be actively individuated by reversing the hierarchy.

The question of domain general versus specific ensemble processing discussed in Section 3.1 can be reframed as a matter of when in the implicit feedforward hierarchy information was initially accrued and the extent to which the hierarchy must be reversed to retrieve relevant aspects. In this view, it is not surprising that studies have repeatedly found correlations between observers' abilities to average low-level features in simple displays and higher-level categorical information, but disparate results for low- and high-level summaries. Although the average representation is accessed in all cases, correlations occur during common-level processing in the initial feedforward implicit sweep.

Reverse hierarchy theory also helps to reconcile seemingly discrepant reports of correlated performance for explicit and implicit measures of mean and variance, versus uncorrelated performance in numerosity and mean estimation and mean numerosity and variability. Whereas the hierarchy must be reversed to recover numerosity information distinct from ensemble representations, mean and variance information can be accessed directly from the higher-level summaries (see Anobile et al., 2014). Finally, reports of uncorrelated estimates for high-level set representations likely arise from having to reverse-navigate the hierarchy to untangle different characteristics of complex sets versus correlated performance when quickly accessing basic ensemble properties. These conclusions also align with reports of limited capacity for representing one feature from one set and a different feature from another set, different statistical descriptors from multiple sets, but parallel access within the same set (Section 2.6).

In the context of RHT, the question of whether qualitatively different mechanisms are involved in ensemble versus individual object representation (Section 3.2.1) also becomes a question of when information is accessed. Ensembles hierarchically generated over implicit feedforward processing can be accessed rapidly, whereas explicit feedback processing is necessary to recover constituent individual item details retained with varying levels of precision depending on the conditions under which they were encoded. In this view, it seems more parsimonious that all or most elements are encoded in a rudimentary manner, versus an explicit bottom-up selection process that purposefully subsamples and encodes individual objects to pass on to a secondary averaging mechanism. Furthermore, having to engage explicit feedback processing to recover details encoded during earlier feedforward implicit processing stages not only helps to explain why numerous studies have reported superior performance in averaging versus membership tasks but why individual item discrimination is not a function of the number of items sampled in simulated performance. A high-level representation accumulated over implicit feedforward processing also fits with findings discussed in Section 3.2.2 that increasing the number of items in the ensemble leads to more precise ensemble representations, and with theoretical accounts such as Baek and Chong's (2020a) distributed attention model. This high-level representation persists even when the hierarchy cannot be reversed for explicit access to individual representations (Section 3.2.3), such as when focused attention is withdrawn, depleted, or conscious perception of individual objects is otherwise prevented. This implicit feedforward and explicit feedback determination aids in understanding the sparing of ensemble perception from deficits seen in conditions such as neglect and ASD.

Reverse hierarchy theory proposes ensemble representations are constructed over feedforward implicit processing, making the perception of constituent individual elements unnecessary, but not necessarily uninfluential. In line with findings discussed in Section 3.3, elements crowded from perceptual awareness are included in ensemble representations, but not explicitly recoverable when the hierarchy is reversed. Similarly, the retinal image of the ensemble is subject to context-based rescaling over implicit feedforward processing. It is also parsimonious to assume when initial encoding of individual items is biased such that some are encoded more precisely, foveally, or selectively attended, their contribution to the overall ensemble representation may be amplified, but items too dissimilar are not integrated into this later-stage robust representation. Finally, ensemble representations are directly accessed, without the need to reverse the hierarchy to mathematically combine separate representations of sum and quantity.

Although high-level ensemble representations are obligatory (Section 3.4), as the starting point of conscious perception in our framework, it is often possible to retrieve information about at least some individual elements. As discussed further in Section 5.6, intelligent perceptual strategies should allow for this option of fidelity when resources are available and performance would benefit. Yet, individual representations are not as robust when reverse-accessed compared to higher-order ensemble descriptors. As discussed further in Section 5.4, this greater reliance on higher-level ensemble representation likely underlies our ability to perceive the surrounding environment as complete and coherent versus a bombardment of discrete, discordant, bits. Although false alarms to the mean and other ensemble effects that skew individual item perception can be seen as "detrimental" to veridical performance, this sort of global processing allows for the perception of information in context. Perception naturally unfolds within the context of our surroundings. Therefore, conscious perception should logically be grounded in contextual representations.

Overall, RHT helps to bridge many gaps in our understanding of how ensemble encoding is accomplished, resolving numerous seemingly discrepant results. In addition to this theoretical framework, we next discuss plausible neural mechanisms for ensemble encoding.

4 Neural Mechanisms

Reverse hierarchy theory provides a cohesive, neurally plausible description of ensemble encoding. Before discussing potential neural models, we briefly review attempts to "localize" ensemble encoding in the brain. The lack of definitive results is not surprising if ensemble encoding is understood in the context of a distributed, hierarchical, bidirectional processing network. Along these lines, we turn to a discussion of developing population-coding models of ensemble encoding.

4.1 Neuroimaging

The neural substrates involved in ensemble representations remain poorly understood. Although Cant and Xu (2012) localized adaptation activation specific to photos of "ensembles" (e.g., fruit) different from surface textures with similar low-level properties to the parahippocampal cortex, their study did not include a measure of ensemble encoding. Therefore, results can only be interpreted as evidence for unique activation in global processing of sets of objects versus lower-level textural processing. In a subsequent behavioral study also without a measure of ensemble encoding, changing unattended features of sets impaired observers' abilities to classify the overall set category based on an attended feature, but not to classify the category of a single stimulus that also varied on an irrelevant feature (Cant et al., 2015). In a later fMRI adaptation paradigm, manipulations of density and ratio had no effect on this parahippocampal area, but activation was modulated by shape and surface properties of individual elements (Cant & Xu, 2017). Although these findings align with reports that texture ensembles selectively activate PPA (e.g., Park & Park, 2017), they are somewhat contrary to reports of improvements of numeric averaging with transcranial magnetic stimulation of parietal cortex (Brezis et al., 2016). Importantly, it will be necessary for future studies to include a task confirming ensemble encoding, as well as to explicitly distinguish between the present discussion of ensemble encoding and the established literature on texture perception.

One recent study by Im and colleagues (2021) directly compared set versus individual object processing using magnetoencephalography (MEG). When observers viewed two sets of four faces with different emotions or two individual faces with different emotions and chose which set or individual to avoid, distinct patterns of earlier dorsal activation for groups and later ventral activation for single faces were observed. These results add to previous proposals (e.g., Ariely, 2001), suggesting dorsal involvement in rapid, parallel-processing of sets, qualitatively distinct from ventral mechanisms involved in individual object encoding. Another recent study by Tark and colleagues (2021) further demonstrated a range of responses selective for average versus item orientation as a function of task-relevance, ranging from early and extrastriate to later frontal regions. Although several factors such as motor response modulated the robustness of these effects, findings support the proposal that ensembles are encoded from pooled population signals at multiple levels throughout the visual information processing hierarchy.

Overall, attempts to localize cortical regions involved in ensemble encoding are inconclusive, likely because ensembles are encoded in a hierarchical manner, over the course of feedforward implicit processing. We suggest a promising route for future studies is to selectively engage implicit feedforward and explicit feedback processing to allow for the classification of unique ensemble versus single-item encoding.

4.2 Population Coding

Several theoretical models have been proposed to account for performance on a range of different ensemble tasks (Section 3). However, few have explicated underlying neural substrates or implemented computational models. Another promising direction for characterizing the neural underpinnings of ensemble perception is to derive these representations from known basic mechanisms of neural coding, the population responses of feature-selective neurons. Established by Hubel and Wiesel's (1959, 1962) seminal work, neurons of sensory cortical regions are selectively tuned to particular feature values. Usually, neurons respond preferentially over a range of values, such that curves can be obtained by measuring the neuron's response as a function of stimulus feature values. In simple cases, the tuning function is approximated by a unimodal function with its peak at the neuron's "preferred" feature value. Measuring various neuronal responses within the same receptive field (RF) returns tuning curves with peaks at different feature values, describing a broad spectrum of feature preferences. When a stimulus is presented within a given RF, the responses of neurons within the RF are modulated in accordance with their tuning curves and this distribution of responses is the *population neural code*. Various rules can be applied to decode a single feature value from the population response, such as peak activation (e.g., Yantis & Abrams, 2014), vectorization (e.g., Georgopoulos et al., 1986), and whole population Bayesian decoding (e.g., Ma et al., 2006).

Given ubiquity across modalities and feature spaces, population coding is a straightforward means for building a broad range of ensemble representations. A handful of previous studies have described how population encoding may theoretically account for ensemble encoding. Haberman and Whitney (2012) briefly outlined a plausible neural mechanism to achieve joint population code for spatial ensembles through pooling of multiple responses from local populations with small RF's by neurons with large RF's. As RF size tends to steadily increase from lower to higher levels of neural processing, spatial pooling and ensemble representation appear to be natural results of feedforward processing. Brezis and colleagues (2018) further suggested a computational neural-network model of averaging using joint population code based on observers' performance averaging over RSVP-sequences of two-digit numbers (Section 2.1.8). Each number produced a noisy Gaussian-shaped population response in the first encoding layer (L1). A second layer (L2) then decoded the average, such that each L2 neuron was also a number-selective neuron with a broad tuning curve determining the synaptic weights of each L1 neuron. Therefore, the output of each L2 neuron was the sum of L1 neurons' excitations multiplied by their synaptic weights, and average number was decoded as L2 population peak activation. This model accounted for behavioral data in a number averaging task but has yet to be extended to other features or statistical properties.

Whereas Brezis et al.'s (2018) model uses a pooling layer only for decoding the average from the joint response of local number-selective neural populations, Utochkin, Choi, and Chong (in review) shifted the focus to the pooled population response as the *actual neural representation of the ensemble* (Figure 8). Their model provides a simple explanation for how the mean feature is encoded directly from feedforward-pooling of the whole display by a large RF. The width of the pooled response can be directly decoded as variability, and the entire shape of the pooled population code is isomorphic to the distribution of the physical stimulus properties, conveying a range of useful information in addition to the mean using the same code, without a devoted decoding mechanism to readout the shape.

Utochkin and colleagues' population response model successfully predicted performance previously reported in a range of 2AFC orientation (Dakin, 2001; Solomon, 2010; Yashiro et al., 2020), size (Baek & Chong, 2020a; Solomon et al., 2011), motion direction (Watamaniuk et al., 1989), and color (Virtanen et al., 2020) averaging tasks, method of adjustment orientation (Epstein et al., 2020; Utochkin & Brady, 2020) and size (Khvostov & Utochkin, 2019; Kim & Chong, 2020) averaging tasks, orientation variance discrimination tasks (Jeong & Chong, 2021), as well as implicit feature distribution learning based on local changes of the underlying probability density (Chetverikov et al., 2016, 2017; Hansmann-Roth et al., 2021). Along these lines, AAEs to summary statistics (Section 2.5) can also be explained via shifts in joint population codes induced by neural fatigue after long exposure to an ensemble adaptor.

Utochkin and colleagues' population response model provides a neurally plausible basis for RHT. Hierarchical, implicit feedforward processing in bottom layers is directly readout at higher levels, and explicit feedback connections not only access but can reweight bottom layer representations. Baek and Chong (2020b) suggest an important extension of a population-based neural

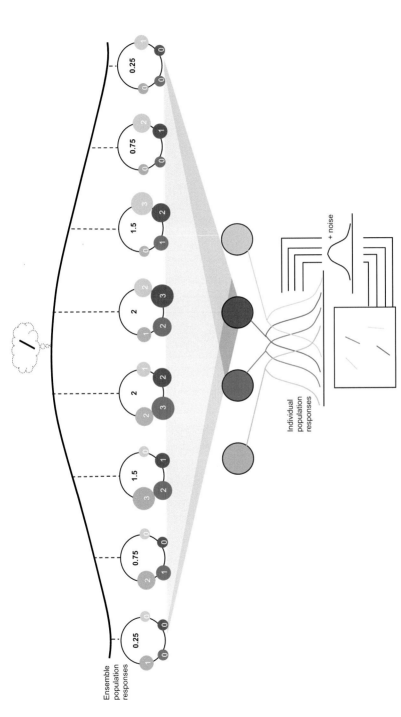

Figure 8 Principal architecture of Utochkin and colleagues' population-coding model, illustrating responses of two layers to a set of four differently oriented lines. The bottom layer produces four noisy population responses in separate small RFs (large colored circles). Top layer neurons pool signals from all local RF's in accordance with their synaptic weights (numbers in four smaller colored circles) and return the normalized average (numbers in large unfilled circles). The top layer distribution of output signals is the model's neural representation of the ensemble.

mechanism where attention is distributed by applying a broadly tuned Gaussian filter to the joint population code, favoring the overall mean representation and effectively "washing-out" individual representations. In contrast, attention is focused by applying a sharply tuned Gaussian filter to a local population response, biasing the representation of an attended item. Utochkin and colleagues' model also provides a straightforward mechanism of easy outlier detection and robust averaging via detection of discontinuity in the population code if the outlier is strongly dissimilar from other items, or by feedback normalization of population responses to individual stimuli from joint population activity. "False-alarms to the mean" result from the population response smoothing the differences between the underlying distributions and thus boosting representation in the center. Furthermore, the joint population code also provides a straightforward mechanistic explanation of the "math" behind estimation of ensemble statistics, where mean is directly calculated.

Overall, the lack of concrete findings regarding the neural substrates of ensemble encoding is not surprising in the context of our RHT/pooled-population account. Distributed, hierarchical encoding in lower layers accrued over implicit feedforward processing is accessed directly from pooled responses in higher layers. Explicit feedback to lower layers is necessary to retrieve individual representations, which are modulated by the fidelity of encoding and feedback from higher layers.

5 Foundational Processing

Given our account can effectively explain a range of findings in the ensemble perception literature, we next consider the implications and applications of this theoretical and mechanistic framework. Our view implies ensemble encoding emerges as a natural process from implicit feedforward processing within a limited-capacity system, distinct from, but influenced by processes governing individual item encoding. Somewhat contrary to previous proposals, our account predicts ensemble encoding is a fundamental process versus a supplementary process to overcome focused attentional processing limitations. Gist-based ensemble perception is the foundation of all sensory processing, necessary for detailed encoding, canceling noise contaminating individual item representations, allowing for efficient storage, categorization, segmentation, and perceptual learning of incoming sensory information while maintaining spatiotemporal perceptual stability. In contrast to traditional theoretical proposals starting with object features, we argue ensemble properties are the building blocks of perception, permitting the majority of the world to be rapidly interpreted, only later to be investigated in detail by more effortful, explicit, focused-attentional processing.

5.1 Rapid and Efficient

5.1.1 Gist

Gist perception is a first approximation or best guess at integrating bottom-up information, prior to checking for inner consistency or confirmation from prior knowledge (e.g., Hochstein, 2020). Though we often believe we know the details of a scene, there is a vast amount of evidence that we miss most and require prolonged scrutiny to build a more individuated representation of scene elements (e.g., Cohen & Chun, 2017). Summarizing complex scenes by rapidly forming statistical descriptions of sets of similar items allows for economical description without individuating each member (Ariely, 2001). Our account divides perception into two categories: (1) rapid, *vision-at-a-glance* global perception of the scene accrued over implicit feedforward processing and readout directly from higher-layer pooled population responses, versus (2) slower, *vision-with-scrutiny*, depending on explicit feedback processing via serial scanning of local areas or top-down reverse hierarchy return to lower cortical areas where details are represented (Hochstein & Ahissar, 2002).

There is broad evidence for this dichotomy, beginning with the discrepancy between severe limits to attention and a rich, detailed representation of the visual scene. The span of apprehension is limited to three to four items (Woodworth, 1938), and change detection can take many seconds (Rensink et al., 1997). Yet, gist is rapidly perceived (e.g., Potter & Faulconer, 1975; Torralba et al., 2006) and instances of a category can be detected with little cost to simultaneous attention-demanding tasks (Li et al., 2002; Thorpe et al., 1996). This dichotomy is repeated between the speed of parallel visual search for single features independent of set size, versus serial search for conjunctions of features, or absent features, linearly dependent on set size (Treisman & Gelade, 1980; Treisman & Gormican, 1988).

Recently pointed out by Raidvee and colleagues (2020), Kahneman (2011) advanced an intriguing idea about constraints imposed upon visual processing, proposing the average length of randomly positioned lines can be judged with considerable accuracy, but the total length of these lines cannot (in line with findings discussed in Sections 3.3.5 and 4.2). Accordingly, the mean feature of a collection of similar geometric figures can be computed by an evolutionarily old system producing rapid, parallel, and automatic analysis with only the final product accessible to conscious awareness. An evolutionarily more recent system performs slowly, using sequential processes typical of deliberate thinking. Unlike accounts of ensemble encoding considering how summary representations may subserve processes responsible for individual item representations (e.g., Alvarez, 2011), or be carried out by separate neural substrates (e.g., Cohen et al., 2016), our account similarly starts with gist-based ensemble representation as the most basic, fundamental form of perception. In line with Kahneman's (2011) proposal, vision-with-scrutiny via focused attention is the supplemental process, facilitating goal-directed actions and highlighting salient targets which cannot happen unless basic, feedforward, implicit processing has given rise to ensemble gist-based representation.

5.1.2 Noise Cancellation

Whereas many computational attempts to represent visual information aim to produce exact replicas of the input stimulus and minimize information loss, the human visual system is not equipped with the processing or metabolic capacity for such intensive encoding. Ariely (2001) proposed the system instead relies on smart forms of representations like statistical encoding of sets to extract just enough to preserve the important information needed to successfully maintain stable perception necessary to interact within the surrounding environment. Alvarez (2011) further proposed combining samples acts to reduce error by averaging-out independent noise.

Such proposals are well grounded in earlier observations of the visual system's structure and function (Section 1.1), and in line with later findings 2AFC speed estimates relative to a standard stimulus speed were more precise over six smaller patches versus a single larger patch (Verghese & Stone, 1996) and discriminations of average brightness were more precise for sets of twelve discs versus single discs (Takano & Kimura, 2020). Sun and Chong (2020) provided empirical evidence averaging acts to reduce noise. Observers' judgments of which side of a display of four different faces relative to a single neutral face on the opposite side of the display appeared angrier were less impaired by inverting displays than judgments between two single faces. In line with Baek and Chong's (2020a) proposal (Section 3.2.2; Figure 3d–f), noise cancellation is a natural result of the pooled population response. Similarly, in our framework, input noise is averaged out in the pooled population response accumulated over implicit feedforward processing. The population response therefore provides a "compressed" summary representation of the ensemble that can be rapidly accessed and is less corrupted by non-systematic noise inherent in lower-level item representations. As discussed further in Section 5.7.2, this efficient noise-canceling compression can even be extended to real-world situations where multiple independent estimates are combined within limited pools of observers.

Relying on ensemble representations resulting from pooled population responses accumulated over implicit feedforward processing allows for rapid perceptions of the gist of the scene. We argue these higher-level representations are the starting point of conscious perception, such that rapid access to ensemble and gist information allows us to quickly and efficiently see the "forest" without having to expend the energy to reverse the hierarchy and reconstruct it based on noisy individual "trees."

5.2 Working Memory

Storing information in working memory is a highly demanding capacity-limited process (Cowan, 2001; Luck & Vogel, 1997). Increasing the number of to-be-stored items quickly leads to substantial information loss (Wilken & Ma, 2004). Ensemble representation has typically been thought of as a tool to cope with these severe limitations (e.g., Alvarez, 2011). Instead, we propose it is a fundamental form of hierarchical representation, driving rapid, gist-based conscious perception well before individual item representations can be explicitly accessed. There is mounting evidence individual item representations are recovered as a function of ensemble properties, even when this may lead to false memories. Warping toward top-level ensemble representations when retrieving noisily encoded lower-level item representations is a means of perceiving individual objects in context.

5.2.1 Hierarchical Encoding

There is a growing collection of evidence that ensemble representations affect memories of constituent items. Brady and Alvarez (2011) asked observers to memorize the sizes of two of three color-defined spatially intermixed sets of three dots each, then adjust the size of a dot to the remembered size in a given location. Observers' memories of the same physically sized dots were systematically biased toward the average size of all three dots of a particular color, but only when they had to ignore a third color set. Although results were interpreted as observers averaging only when color was task-relevant, set size also decreased when only two sets were presented (Section 5.6). Lew and Vul (2013, 2015) similarly found observers remembered locations of up to eight objects organized into spatially distinct clusters with bias toward the central cluster location, such that errors were more correlated with the central location than actual item locations. Walker and Vul (2014) reported a somewhat related "cheerleader effect," with individual faces rated as more attractive when presented in groups of up to sixteen faces.

There is also evidence top-down influence of ensemble representations on individual object recall is not restricted to bias toward the mean. Utochkin and Brady (2020) presented observers with displays of four triangles and asked them to adjust a test to the orientation of a single triangle in a pre-cued location, a single triangle at a post-cued location, and the mean orientation of all four triangles. Not only was memory for individual orientations biased toward the mean, but the precision of memory for an individual item increased with decreasing variance and errors more skewed toward mean orientation with narrower ranges. Son and colleagues (2020) reported similar effects for observers' memories of individual item orientation in displays of five tilted bars and color in displays of four color squares. Although error for items within the same cluster was affected by similarity, results may be more indicative of outlier detection (Section 5.3.2) given clusters always consisted of one set of up to four objects and a second set of only one object.

Together, findings are consistent with hierarchical coding in working memory with information about a set of remembered items represented at several levels. Along these lines, Brady and Alvarez (2015) found patterns of errors for item color memory in displays of up to six color circles were best accounted for by a model allowing for representations at multiple levels of abstraction. Given the limits of working memory, this sort of multilevel storage is useful for rapidly accessing higher-level gist-based representations especially when it is not necessary to retrieve details. However, as discussed in Section 4.3.2, and elaborated in Section 5.2.3, this strategy becomes detrimental when fidelity is necessary for remembering individual items.

5.2.3 False Memories and Bias

Perceiving individual objects in context is generally beneficial for coherent, stable perception. However, findings such as "false alarms" to the mean (Section 3.4.2) raise the important question of whether ensemble encoding may ultimately underlie false memories. False memories were originally empirically studied by Deese (1959), later popularized by Roediger and McDermott (1995), using what has come to be called the Deese-Roediger-McDermott (DRM) paradigm. Participants are presented with lists of words and then asked to report words that were present. Typical reports included related but absent words participants were as certain as being presented as other correctly recalled words, especially if the absent word was prototypical of the set (Pardilla-Delgado & Payne, 2017). Such false memories may also occur in a more abstract manner. For example, "Mandela Effects," named after Fiona Broome's false memory of Nelson Mandela dying in prison in the 1980s, was supposedly shared by many other strangers around the world. Similarly, many people (incorrectly) insist the Monopoly Man wears a monocle. Such "Visual Mandela Effects" have only recently become the subject of empirical investigations (e.g., Prasad & Bainbridge, 2021). However, these and more widely studied "DRM false memories" bear at least some resemblance to findings that observers incorrectly remember an item representing the average value of a set of objects being present in sequences of familiar and novel objects (Section 3.4.2) in that the recall of a specific event is biased toward higher-level ensemble context in which it was experienced.

This implicit categorical bias also may play an important role in interpreting the testimonies of victims in a post "#MeToo" era. Importantly, memories of items and events may be "falsely" warped toward a prototypical value, but this has no bearing on whether the item was actually present or the event occurred. False alarms to the prototype may also help explain implicit racial and gender biases. For example, when observers viewed a sequence of photographs of ten black and ten white faces in random order and indicated which was present in a set of eighty faces, they made fewer false alarms and more correct identifications for faces from their own race (Malpass & Kravitz, 1969). Future studies may verify this "own race effect," as a case of warping to the mean of a race of which one is not an exemplar.

Acknowledging and better understanding such biases may even encourage racial and gender equality in our own professions. A study of longitudinal data from the annual meeting of the Vision Sciences Society by Cooper and Radonjić (2016) revealed a 1:8 ratio of female:male nominees for Young Investigator Awards from 2007 to 2015 despite respective ratios of approximately 1:2 and 1:3 in postdoctoral and regular society members. Perhaps individuals were nominated based on similarity to a prototypical candidate, largely constructed from previous predominantly male exemplars. As discussed further in Section 5.4, perceptual learning may underlie both the origin of and solution to such biases, as information accumulated about exemplars shapes perceptions.

From basic-level properties to abstract social constructs, memories and moment-to-moment perceptions are grounded in higher-level categorical and gist-based representations. In our framework, these representations anchor conscious perception, providing the context in which to evaluate individual objects and events. This sort of high-level bias not only warps individual representations toward set properties but can be extended to more complex categorical prototypes.

5.3 Perceptual Organization

Ensemble representations allow for a quick, efficient organization of information into meaningful chunks. In our framework, these gist-based representations are the building blocks of perception, with feedback contextual influence on how we perceive individual objects and events. This account of ensemble encoding promises to be an extremely useful tool for explaining how pooled population responses may organize incoming sensory signals into meaningful perceptual units.

5.3.1 Categorization

Utochkin (2015) proposed a simple ensemble-based rule to quickly parse intermixed objects into categories. Given information about the whole feature distribution is available in the joint population code, the shape of this distribution can be categorized by peaks where similar features are concentrated and valleys where the range of reasonable feature variation within a category ends (Figure 9). If features are distributed smoothly along a range with no substantial discontinuity, the ensemble likely represents a single category (Figure 9a). However, if the distribution has several distinct peaks, the number of peaks corresponds to the number of distinct categories (Figure 9b). In this framework, the underlying mechanism of categorization depends on prototypes (mean) and boundaries (range). A plausible neural basis for such categorization is given by single-cell activity of neurons selective to motion direction recorded in monkeys watching two overlapping textures moving in two different directions (Treue et al., 2000). When the angular difference

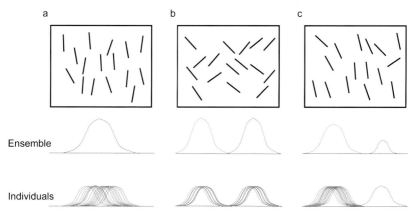

Figure 9 Joint population code for categorization and outlier detection. (a) When features are smoothly distributed over a range, the joint population response contains a single peak representing a single category. (b) When the distribution is discontinuous, it will have multiple peaks corresponding to the number of distinct categories (two in this example). (c) When there is a wide valley between multiple responses and a single outlier response, the set population code reflects the mean of the distribution discounting the outlier, which is represented by a separate population code.

between directions was relatively small, the shape of the population response was a single peak with a maximum at the average direction between the physically presented directions. However, when the angular separation became large, the population response split into two peaks corresponding to the physically presented directions.

There is mounting behavioral evidence for such "split peak" effects of feature distributions on subset categorization. For example, Utochkin and Yurevich (2016) (replicated by Cho & Chong, 2019) demonstrated odd-one-out visual search for size or orientation is modulated by distractor distribution. Observers were faster finding a singleton target if distractors had a smooth distribution versus sharp two- or three-peak distributions. In a subsequent study, Utochkin and colleagues (2018) briefly presented observers with patches of sixty-four line segments of different lengths and orientations. Opposite halves of the display were composed of elements from identical distributions but different correlations between distributions. Discriminations of whether the top or bottom of the display had a given relationship and whether the boundary between the two subpatches was horizontal or vertical were poor unless both distributions of length and orientation had two-peaks, suggesting two-peak distributions supported categorical segmentation when observers could pick only long lines (ignoring short ones) and compare average orientations within this subset. Im and colleagues (2021) also reported when observers were briefly shown a set of sixteen uniquely sized dots and asked to categorize a probe as being large or small relative to set median size, categorization was more accurate if the distribution was two-peaked. Furthermore, when observers performed an attentionally demanding oddball detection task at fixation, the amplitude and latency of the visual mismatch negativity (vMMN; an ERP component indexing automatic oddball detection) were modulated by the orientation and length distributions of background elements could that suddenly change sign over the course of trials (Khvostov et al., 2021). These findings provide converging evidence for automatic ensemble-based categorization.

Cha and colleagues (2018) demonstrated categorical discriminability can even modulate visual awareness. Observers were stereoscopically presented with a display of dots in a given color to one eye and a display of dots in a different color to the other eye, and reported how many colors they perceived at any given time. When the colors were similar, participants reported both colors for a longer proportion of time, but were more prone to perceiving only one color when colors became more dissimilar. These patterns suggest the categorical similarity of colors drives fused perception, and categorical dissimilarity induces binocular rivalry.

5.3.2 Outlier Detection

Directly related to categorization and segmentation, ensemble encoding may play a fundamental role in outlier detection. Outliers differing greatly from other elements "pops-out," and are detected rapidly independent of the number of other elements (Treisman & Gelade, 1980). As discussed in Section 3.3.4, such outliers are generally discounted in computations of ensemble representations, which may also serve as a basis for detecting outliers.

Hochstein and colleagues (2018) directly tested the relationship between averaging and outlier detection. Observers viewed two arrays of heterogeneously oriented bars with different mean orientations and/or with one array containing a bar with an outlier orientation and (1) discriminated which had the average tilt was more clockwise, or (2) which contained an orientation outlier. Performance in the mean and outlier detection tasks was assessed as a function of array variance, the difference in mean orientation between the arrays, and outlier orientation. Overall, performance in the mean task was governed by the difference in mean orientations between the two arrays, independently of the variances, contrary to earlier findings for much smaller (Rosenholtz, 2001). Furthermore, whereas participants could easily discriminate between the mean orientations of arrays even when their distributions largely overlapped, outlier detection performance depended only on the distance of the outlier from the edge of the array. Taken together, these patterns suggest variance only affects outlier detection by determining the range of the set distribution and the outlier must be clearly outside this range to be detected.

As demonstrated in Figure 9c, these characteristics of outlier detection are consistent with the population code analysis (Section 4.2). In this example, the joint population response has a vector sum at the veridical mean of the set only if the outlier is discounted. This discounting is derived from the wide valley at noise level between the responses to the set of counterclockwise orientations and the response to the clockwise outlier. The depth of the valley depends only on the distance of the outlier from the edge of the set's range. A separate population code for the outlier gives its "mean" as the single orientation.

In our framework, ensemble encoding is a crucial mechanism underlying perceptual organization, rapid categorization, and pop out outlier detection. Individual items must be similar enough in some dimension to be included in the same pooled population response. Likewise, items outside the set's range are discounted from the pooled response and represented by a separate population response. These higher-level ensemble representations act as the starting point for conscious perception, actuating swift and efficient categorization and outlier detection.

5.4 Perceptual Learning and Stability

When discussing the relationships between ensemble encoding in categorization, outlier detection, and exemplar representation, an understanding of how ensemble information is accrued over time is an important consideration. Given the structure and redundancy in the surrounding environment, ensemble encoding provides scaffolding for making sense of the constant influx of sensory information. Along these lines, several studies have investigated how the stability of ensemble information over space and time influences perception.

Although perception is modulated by a constant interplay between observer and environmental coordinate systems as we interact within our dynamic surroundings, we nonetheless maintain a general sense of spatiotemporal stability. In our framework, ensemble representations stabilize perception by minimizing disruption from noisy low-level individual item representations and increasing gist-based predictability. If ensemble representations underlie spatiotemporal stability, they should transfer over multiple spatial reference frames. Corbett and Melcher (2014b) first demonstrated ensemble representations translate across eye movements, in retinotopic, spatiotopic, and hemispheric reference frames, and even transfer interocularly. Observers adapted to two side-by-side patches of differently sized circles with small and large mean sizes while remaining centrally fixated and judged which of two subsequently presented tests was larger in the retinotopic, spatiotopic, hemispheric, and interocular conditions displayed in Figure 10. Across all conditions, an AAE persisted such that observers judged the test dot presented in the region adapted to the large mean size set as smaller than the same-sized test dot presented in the small-mean-adapted region. Results provide strong support for the proposal that ensemble representations anchor and unify perception fluctuating between otherwise disparate spatial reference frames.

Studies by Gillen and Heath (2014a, b) extended our understanding of how ensemble information guides perception over eye movements. Over hundreds of trials, they asked participants to make prosaccades toward proximal, middle, and distal targets or antisaccades to mirror locations on the opposite side of the display. In the control condition, targets were either presented in different locations with equal frequency. In the proximal-weighted and distal-weighted conditions, targets were presented five times more frequently in the proximal and distal locations, respectively. Prosaccades were unaffected by unequal weightings, suggesting they were veridically governed by retinotopic information, whereas (relative to the control condition) antisaccades significantly undershot targets in the proximal-weighted condition and overshot in the distal-weighted condition, suggesting ensemble representations governed these volitional movements.

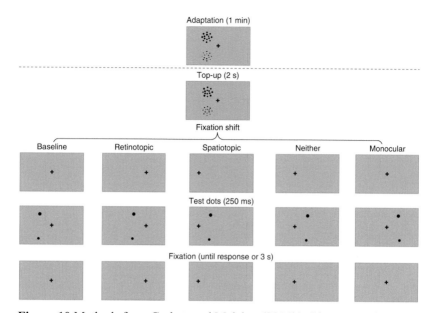

Figure 10 Methods from Corbett and Melcher (2014b). Observers adapted to two patches of dots, one with the larger mean size on the top and bottom of the display. Then, while either maintaining central fixation or shifting fixation, they determined which of two tests appeared larger. In the baseline condition, fixation remained central, and tests appeared at the top and bottom of the locations previously occupied by the adapting patches. In the retinotopic condition, fixation shifted to the opposite side of the display and tests appeared above and below the previous location of central fixation. In the spatiotopic condition, fixation shifted to the opposite side of the screen and tests remained in the spatial locations previously occupied by the adapting displays. In neither condition, fixation shifted to the adapted side of the display and tests shifted to the top and bottom of the vertical meridian. In the monocular condition, displays were presented stereoscopically such that adapting patches were presented to one eye and tests to the other eye, but both appeared to be centrally aligned.

These results help to explain how we can make veridical eye movements to targets while also under the influence of a contextually driven representation of the environment.

To examine how ensemble information may similarly influence the manner in which information is perceived over time, Corbett and Melcher (2014b) next presented observers with displays of sixty-four differently sized Gabors in random horizontal orientations and asked them to search for a single target Gabor tilted from vertical and indicate its clockwise or counterclockwise orientation.

The mean size of the entire display either remained the same over several consecutive trials (stable blocks) or changed on every trial (unstable blocks), but individual Gabor sizes varied randomly on all trials. Not only did observers correctly identify the tilt of the target faster as mean size became stable over time, but they also made faster and fewer eye movements and shorter fixations compared to unstable baseline trials. Further confirmation for this stability effect is given by Manassi and colleagues' (2017) findings that estimates of the mean orientation of displays of nine Gabors were serially dependent (Section 5.7.2). Tong and colleagues (2015) observed a similar effect of the stability of mean luminance in displays of many square patches on the perception of patch variance. Future studies will likely uncover links between statistical stability, the limited temporal window over which ensemble information is updated (Section 2.3), and the temporal dynamics of the implicit feedforward and explicit feedback processing outlined in Section 3.5. Together, results suggest statistical stability allows for rapid efficient outlier detection. Suddenly disrupting stability acts as an unconscious signal of salient change outside the focus of attentional scrutiny, slowing search for individual targets while the system recalibrates to global gist. Such alerting may underlie the feeling of "mindsight" (Rensink, 2004) where observers sense a change without the corresponding visual experience.

This anchoring of perception to ensemble representations is likely a result of perceptually learning the overall shape of internal feature probability distributions over time. Along these lines, Chetverikov and colleagues (2017) used an array of differently oriented bars, asking participants to find an outlier orientation (Section 2.4.3). They trained using a consistent distribution of distractor orientations, and an outlier target orientation over a streak of several trials, and then tested learning by shifting the distractor distribution around a new mean and redefining the target within the original distractor distribution. Target detection speed slowed as a function of the current target orientation's distance from the mean of the prior distractor orientations, and this negative priming effect on search speed generally followed the shape of the preceding distractor distribution. When distractor distributions were bimodal, observers initially performed as if they were uniform and needed more repetitions to show search effects consistent with bimodal preceding distributions. Moerel and colleagues (2016) also found observers initially relied most on parafoveal input when discriminating whether a patch of sixty-three differently oriented Gabors was more clockwise relative to the orientation of a homogeneously oriented reference patch, but estimates expanded peripherally over the course of learning. Taken together, results suggest observers do not have strong initial priors and quickly learn simple distributions, but can flexibly adjust representations to more complex distributions as information accumulates over time.

Within our framework, this sort of ensemble-based learning occurs at higher cortical levels, guiding later, lower-level explicit feedback processing. One way of localizing this sort of perceptual learning is by measuring the degree to which effects are specific versus transferable. If learning modifies representations at lower levels, effects will not transfer to different tasks accomplished by different specific untrained neuronal populations. However, if learning happens at higher-level broadly tuned population responses, effects should transfer to new tasks. To our knowledge there has only been one investigation whether improvement from ensemble perceptual learning transfers across tasks. Hochstein and Pavlovskaya (2020) presented observers with two arrays of heterogeneously-oriented bars with different mean orientations and/or a bar with an outlier orientation and asked them to discriminate the mean orientations or detect the outlier (Section 5.3.2). Participants first performed one of the two tasks for several blocks, then switched to the other task. As expected, training improved both accuracy and speed for both mean discrimination and outlier detection. More importantly, reaction time improvements in the first task transferred to the second task in all cases. Although improvements in accuracy only transferred from outlier detection to mean discrimination, results nonetheless provide some support for our proposal that ensemble-based learning occurs at higher-level broadly tuned populations, which feedback to influence subsequent lower-level processing.

Overall, this collection of work suggests ensemble encoding plays a fundamental role in maintaining spatiotemporal stability. Given the constantly changing retinal image, the visual system likely relies on learning statistical regularities inherent in the surrounding environment to smoothly sew perception together over space and time while allowing for the detection of salient objects and events. Future studies will likely uncover more ways in which the spatiotemporal stability of ensemble representations implicitly governs our interactions with the surrounding environment.

5.5 Heuristic Representation

There is mounting evidence ensemble encoding is part of a broader set of heuristics underlying our ability to rapidly make sense of the dynamic surrounding environment. Studies investigating, "What makes a set a set?" have helped to link ensemble encoding to a larger class of information processing heuristics, namely Gestalt Laws of Perceptual Organization (e.g., Wertheimer, 1923). Along these lines, both ensemble encoding and Gestalt Laws predicate perception on parsimony and recurrent order in the physical world.

Im and Chong (2014) first explicated the link between these forms of heuristic representation, demonstrating Gestalt grouping by spatial proximity and contrast facilitate average size encoding. Observers viewed displays of up to five sets of five circles then estimated the average size of a probed subset. When sets were spatially intermixed and only defined by contrast similarity (similar to Brady & Alvarez, 2011), estimates of subset average size were less precise than when sets were also spatially segregated (by proximity). Corbett (2017) next tested the proposal that Gestalt grouping and perceptual averaging functionally boost capacity of VSTM. Observers were presented with study displays of sixteen dots (well beyond VSTM capacity) for either 500 ms or 5 s and asked to memorize their sizes. Dots were organized into two large- and small-mean size groups of eight defined solely by a Gestalt grouping factor (proximity, similarity, connectedness, common region). Observers adjusted the sizes of six tests to the remembered sizes in the corresponding study locations. In line with previous findings for smaller set sizes defined by similarity and proximity (Brady & Alvarez, 2011; Im & Chong, 2014), observers' memories of individual dots were biased toward Gestalt-defined mean size such that the same size test dot was remembered as larger when presented in the large versus small Gestalt-defined mean size set. Also in line with Lew and Vul's (2015) findings, observers made more similar errors for test dots in the same versus different Gestalt-defined sets. Finally, observers' errors relative to the mean size of the Gestalt-defined group in which a test dot was presented were significantly lower than errors relative to the actual sizes of corresponding dots. Collectively, results imply Gestalt grouping and perceptual averaging warp individual item representations to minimize the error with which individual items are recalled.

Further support for the idea that ensembles are defined by grouping principles is given by findings that observers ignore elements of spatially aligned contours (good continuation) when estimating the average orientation of a patch of elements (Cha & Chong, 2018). Along these lines, Akyuz and colleagues (2018) demonstrated grouping by color similarity facilitates processing of dynamic displays at the set level. Somewhat akin to tracking the movements of soccer players, observers were less able to track the number of times any colored circle "player" gained possession of a soccer ball over an entire group of differently colored players than they were to count the possessions by a given color team, and this ability improved when the same number of players were grouped into fewer color teams with more individual members per team.

Overall, results provide support of our proposal that implicit feedforward processing acts to capitalize on structure and redundancy, employing heuristic grouping and statistical representation strategies. As outlined in Section 5.1.1, this form of hierarchical representation allows for rapid gist-based perception, accrued implicitly over feedforward processing to guide the explicit retrieval and further encoding of incoming sensory information.

5.6 "Smart" Perception

Although we propose higher-order gist-based ensemble information is the starting point of conscious perception, it is not the sole factor. Parsimonious perception should rely on the most relevant information available. As noted throughout this Element, numerous studies of ensemble encoding have used displays with only a few unique items. However, when individual item representations are task-relevant and can be recovered from explicit feedback processing, intelligent perception should instead be reliant on this detailed information versus more immediately available ensemble representations.

New evidence suggests heuristic perceptual strategies are indeed employed in such a "smart" manner. Using an established ERP-index of VSTM capacity, the contralateral delay activity (CDA), Corbett and colleagues (osf.io/e3dvq; Figure 11) explicitly tested how Gestalt-grouping and perceptual averaging affect memory capacity as a function of whether the to-be-remembered information exceeds the typical four-item limit. Although CDA amplitude increases as the set size of a to-be-remembered display increases (Vogel & Machizawa, 2004), this has typically been used with displays of only a few items. Adapting Corbett's (2017) methods into a CDA paradigm not only allowed for a critical test of whether grouping and averaging decrease VSTM load, but also whether this occurs even when it would not be beneficial. Preliminary results replicate Corbett's (2017) previous behavioral findings with individual items in displays of sixteen dots remembered as a function of Gestalt-group mean size. However, this behavioral index was not observed for displays of only four dots. Furthermore, CDA amplitudes significantly decreased for grouped versus ungrouped displays of sixteen dots but not for grouped versus ungrouped displays of four dots, and CDA amplitudes for grouped displays of sixteen dots were significantly lower than for corresponding groups of only four dots. Convergent behavioral and EEG results provide strong evidence grouping and averaging function in an intelligent manner, maximizing information in compressed representations when capacity for individual representation is exceeded but not at the expense of fidelity when individual representations can be explicitly recovered.

These results suggest ensemble encoding is part of a "smart" perceptual processing system, mediating between the needs to attend to salient objects and events while maintaining a sense of perceptual stability. Importantly, these considerations must be factored into the design of future studies of ensemble encoding and results from studies using displays of only a few unique items should not be considered as indicative of ensemble encoding. These findings may also account for several discrepant findings, for example

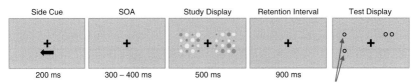

"*Adjust each Test circle on the attended side to match the size of the corresponding circle in the Study display*"

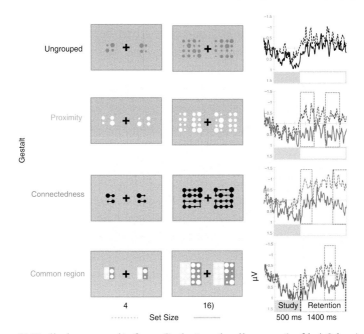

Figure 11 Preliminary results from Corbett and colleagues (osf.io/e3dvq:). Observers adjusted the size of a test to the remembered size in the corresponding study display location. Sets contained either four or sixteen dots, ungrouped, or grouped into two large- and small-mean size sets by proximity, similarity, or common region. Tests in displays of sixteen dots were remembered as a function of Gestalt-group mean size, but adjustments for test dots in display of four dots demonstrated no such mean size bias. Furthermore, CDA amplitudes were lower for grouped versus ungrouped displays of sixteen dots, and CDA amplitudes for displays of sixteen dots were significantly lower than for corresponding Gestalt groups of only four dots.

change detection performance using sets of four colored circles or tilted Gabors was not well approximated by a model that relies on ensemble encoding versus individual objects summation (Harrison et al., 2021). In summary, we assert that reshaping how ensemble representations are involved in perceptual processing and how investigations are executed are critical issues to be addressed in all future work.

5.7 Applied

Besides considerable theoretical implications for human information processing, findings from studies of ensemble encoding can also be abstracted to several real-world situations. As the access point for conscious perception, ensemble representations are an intuitive, rapid means of communicating complex information. Greater reliance on this gist-based heuristic processing may even explain experts' versus algorithms' superior abilities to rapidly detect targets in safety-critical situations.

5.7.1 Data Visualization

Ensemble representations convey a large amount of useful information about sets and are becoming increasingly important for visualization as general statistical practices extend beyond point and interval estimates to whole distributions. Cui and Liu (2021) comprehensively reviewed how difficult-to-understand statistical concepts may be more easily captured in ensemble representations. Szafir and colleagues (2016) suggested a taxonomy of data visualizations tasks linked to various aspects of ensemble perception. Identification includes screening raw data for outliers or searching for a group with an average substantially different than other groups (Section 5.3.2). Summarization of multiple values via descriptive statistics directly relates to ensemble statistics, such as spatial positions along axes. Segmentation involves an ability to parse data into clusters, as in ensemble-based categorization and segmentation (Section 5.3.1). Finally, estimating the structure of data patterns is in many ways analogous to economical ensemble descriptions that facilitate gist perception without needing to individuate items (Section 5.1.1).

Investigations of graphical perception have replicated several fundamental results from ensemble perception studies. For example, Fouriezos and colleagues (2008) reported participants' judgments of the average heights of clusters of bar plot bars were subject to the same range and set size effects observed in ensemble averaging tasks across feature domains (Section 3.2.2). Similarly, correlation discrimination follows fundamental laws of perception, such that just noticeable differences between two scatterplots increase in proportion to the absolute distance from one, conforming to Weber's Law (Harrison et al., 2014; Rensink & Baldridge, 2010). Rensink (2017) asked participants to determine which of two side-by-side scatter plots were more correlated and to adjust a test plot until its perceived correlation was at the midpoint between two reference points. Discrimination performance increased as a linear function of the difference between the depicted correlations, and the magnitude of the perceived correlation grew as a log function of the correlation, suggesting an abstract statistic of information entropy underlies correlation perception providing a rapid global impression of apparent order. A later comparative study by Yang and colleagues (2018) clarified other basic features such as area of the dot cloud and variance in distances of individual dots from the trend line also contribute to rapid correlation perception.

On the contrary, some findings from visualization perception studies are not predicted by ensemble perception. For example, although observers intuitively capture the mean of various features (Section 2.1), they misconceive central tendency when reading histograms (e.g., mistaking the highest bar as the mode; Cui & Liu, 2021). Given observers are usually better at estimating averages than totals (Section 3.3.5), Yuan and colleagues' (2019) findings that observers relied on the total area of bar clusters when judging mean height are also surprising. Overall, data visualization is a complex phenomenon, clearly not limited to rough ensemble representations yet likely subserved by at least a subset of the same basic perceptual mechanisms.

5.7.2 "Wisdom of Ensembles"

Ideas from the ensemble perception literature can also be abstracted to potentially solve a range of real-world safety-critical problems. For example, findings that the limited capacity visual system averages estimates to boost precision and decrease noise (Section 5.1.2) align with the "wisdom of crowds." Galton (1907) first noted the average of 787 individuals' estimates of the weight of an ox was closer to the actual value than any individual's estimate. This power of averaging has also been studied in the context of "the crowd within" individual observers. Vul and Pashler (2008) asked observers to make two different estimates about real-world knowledge (e.g., "What percentage of the world's airports are in the United States?") either within the same session or separated by a three-week delay. When a given observer's estimates were averaged, those made with a three-week delay were significantly more precise owing to increased independence from the temporal delay. Corbett and colleagues (2011) further tested whether this sort of boost from independence applied to a given observer's estimates of numerosity of patches of dots in an n-back paradigm. When an individual's estimates of the same numerosity were averaged, the average became more precise the further apart in time estimates were made. These results parallel the visual system's intelligent approach of averaging redundant information to increase precision and decrease noise.

Abstracting from findings that the visual system capitalizes on regularities by sampling the most unique information can lead to innovative approaches to real-world safety-critical problems. For example, since Wolfe and colleagues' (2005) report even experts miss around 30 percent of rare targets (e.g., tumors in mammograms, weapons in baggage scans), there have been countless behavioral and algorithmic attempts to boost detection performance in these critical situations. However, none have approached this question from the standpoint of a limited capacity system (e.g., a small pool of trained baggage scanners or radiologists). Along these lines, Corbett and Munneke (2018) asked observers to make continuous estimates of whether a given image of nine items contained a rare target (a tool as proxy for weapons in baggage scans and a tumor in a mammogram), or a frequent target such a Gabor larger or smaller than all other items. Importantly, observers performed these tasks independently without knowledge their performance would be combined. Their estimates in the rare target tasks were then paired based on the most decorrelated patterns of performance in the basic Gabors tasks, yielding up to a 22 percent increase in signal detection in the rare target tasks. Considering findings that serial dependence introduces systematic bias in individual radiologists' judgments (Manassi et al., 2021), this boost in detection from pairing judgments based on maximally decorrelated individual differences sharply underscores the power of averaging when there is a limited capacity for individual sampling.

Overall, intelligent strategies like ensemble encoding emerge from the limited capacity human information processing system with important implications for maximizing performance in many real-world tasks. As our understanding of ensemble encoding's fundamental role in human information processing expands, so will the potential for such applications. Importantly, computational approaches, including artificial intelligence may never fully approximate human information processing unless starting from this limited-capacity standpoint. Strategies like ensemble encoding can be "built-in" to existing systems. Yet, without necessitating such heuristics, the perhaps unlimited number of human perceptual abilities yet to be uncovered will not likely naturally emerge from an artificial system.

By capitalizing on structure and redundancy inherent in the surrounding environment, statistical representations provide efficient means for rapidly getting the gist of noisy sensory inputs. This summary processing gives rise to our ability to rapidly detect outliers, group and categorize information. Learning regularities in sensory input provides a means of mediating between the needs to maintain stable perception in an ever-dynamic environment while still being able to detect salient changes. This "smart" perception is an emergent heuristic of our limited capacity information processing system and may explain why humans exceed the performance of even the most advanced algorithmic approaches in a range of real-world situations.

6 Conclusions

Ensemble encoding is ubiquitous in human information processing, with potentially an unlimited number of features summarized by different statistical
descriptors across multiple sensory modalities. Considering the basic perceptual nature of ensemble encoding and substantial evidence it operates over both
space and time, the potential function roles of efficient summary encoding will
likely also continue to grow as we uncover new ways in which statistical
summaries of environmental regularities shape perception.

Although a number of studies have found different attentional manipulations
subsequently modulate ensemble encoding in various ways, these statistical
summaries nonetheless persist even in patients with impaired or alternative
attentional abilities. In fact, no study as of yet has empirically demonstrated
a way to prevent ensemble encoding, even when this is disadvantageous to
performance, can warp memories, or even induce false memories. From this
perspective, ensemble encoding is a distinct, more fundamental process than
attentional scrutiny, allowing for immediate perceptual representations of the
overwhelming majority of information.

We argue ensemble encoding can be best understood within the context of our
RHT/population coding account. In this theoretical and mechanistic framework,
feedforward and feedback connections underscore the pervasiveness of ensemble encoding with representations active at multiple stages of information
processing. Overall, ensemble encoding is a viable mechanism for pooling
samples to compress information and reduce error, seemingly involved in
every aspect of perception from how we rapidly interpret the gist of a scene to
how we remember, categorize, segment, and learn information, underscoring
their basic and fundamental nature, likely to have evolved as part of an older
information processing system in response to regularities inherent in the surrounding environment.

Our proposal that ensemble representations are a fundamental consequence
of a limited capacity system is somewhat contrary to previous proposals that it
functions as a coping mechanism to bypass capacity limitations. Along these
lines, it is necessary to reshape how we think about ensemble encoding not so
much as a mathematical operation, but as a summary form of representation.
Throughout this Element, we have noted numerous discrepant findings stemming from studies using displays of items well within the capacity of focused
attentional processing. Future studies must employ larger set sizes to accurately
inform our understanding of ensemble encoding.

Our knowledge of ensemble encoding has grown exponentially since Ariely
(2001) formalized the conversation. We are only beginning to realize the powerful

and wide-reaching applications. It is our hope that future studies inspired by the collection of ideas in this Element will serve as a springboard for new applications and a scaffolding to strengthen the link between other foundational ideas in perception described over the entire ensemble of work in this Elements in Perception Series.

References

Ahissar, M., & Hochstein, S., (1997). Task difficulty and the specificity of perceptual learning. *Nature*, *387*(6631), 401–406.

Ahissar, M., & Hochstein, S. (2004). The reverse hierarchy theory of visual perceptual learning. *Trends in Cognitive Sciences*, *8*(10), 457–464.

Akyuz, S., Munneke, J., & Corbett, J. E. (2018). Set similarity modulates object tracking in dynamic environments. *Attention, Perception, & Psychophysics*, *80*(7), 1744–1751.

Albrecht, A. R., & Scholl, B. J. (2010). Perceptually averaging in a continuous visual world: Extracting statistical summary representations over time. *Journal of Vision*, *9*(8), 957–957.

Albrecht, A. R., Scholl, B. J., & Chun, M. M. (2012). Perceptual averaging by eye and ear: Computing summary statistics from multimodal stimuli. *Attention, Perception, & Psychophysics*, *74*, 810–815.

Allik, J., Toom, M., Raidvee, A., Averin, K., & Kreegipuu, K. (2013). An almost general theory of mean size perception. *Vision Research*, *83*, 25–39.

Allik, J., Toom, M., Raidvee, A., Averin, K., & Kreegipuu, K. (2014). Obligatory averaging in mean size perception. *Vision Research*, *101*, 34–40.

Alvarez, G. A. (2011). Representing multiple objects as an ensemble enhances visual cognition. *Trends in Cognitive Sciences*, 15 (3), 122–131.

Alvarez G. A., & Oliva, A. (2008). The representation of simple ensemble visual features outside the focus of attention. *Psychological Science*, *19*(4), 392–398.

Alvarez, G. A., & Oliva, A. (2009). Spatial ensemble statistics are efficient codes that can be represented with reduced attention. *Proceedings of the National Academy of Sciences*, *106*(18), 7345–7350.

Anobile, G., Cicchini, G. M., & Burr, D. C. (2014). Separate mechanisms for perception of numerosity and density. *Psychological Science*, *25*(1), 265–270.

Ariely, D. (2001). Seeing sets: Representation by statistical properties. *Psychological Science*, *12*(2), 157–162.

Ariely, D. (2008). Better than average? When can we say that subsampling of items is better than statistical summary representations? *Perception & Psychophysics*, *70*(7), 1325–1326.

Attarha, M., & Moore, C. M. (2014). Orientation summary statistics are limited in processing capacity. *Visual Cognition*, *22*, 1018–1022.

Attarha, M., & Moore, C. M. (2015a). The capacity limitations of orientation summary statistics. *Attention, Perception, & Psychophysics*, 77, 116–1131.

Attarha, M., & Moore, C. M. (2015b). The perceptual processing capacity of summary statistics between and within feature dimensions. *Journal of Vision*, *15*(4), 9, 1–17.

Attarha, M., Moore, C. M., & Vecera, S. (2014). Summary statistics of size: Fixed processing capacity for multiple ensembles but unlimited processing capacity for single ensembles. *Journal of Experimental Psychology: Human Perception and Performance*, *40*(4), 1440–1449.

Attarha, M., Moore, C. M., & Vecera, S. (2016). The time limited statistician: Temporal constraints on the establishment of summary representations. *Journal of Experimental Psychology: Human Perception and Performance*, *42*(10), 1497–1504.

Attneave, F. (1954). Some informational aspects of visual perception. *Psychological Review*, *61*(3), 183–193.

Baek, J., & Chong, S. C. (2020a). Distributed attention model of perceptual averaging. *Attention, Perception, & Psychophysics*, *82*(1), 63–79.

Baek, J., & Chong, S. C. (2020b). Ensemble perception and focused attention: Two different modes of visual processing to cope with limited capacity. *Psychonomic Bulletin & Review*, *27*(4), 602–606.

Barlow, H. B. (1961). Possible principles underlying the transformation of sensory messages. In *Sensory Communication* (p. 217–234). MIT Press.

Bauer, B. (2009). Does Stevens's Power Law for brightness extend to perceptual brightness averaging? *Psychological Record*, *59*, 171–185.

Bauer, B. (2015). A selective summary of visual averaging research and issues up to 2000. *Journal of Vision*, *15*(4), 14, 1–15.

Bauer, B. (2017). Perceptual averaging of line length: Effects of concurrent digit memory load. *Attention, Perception, & Psychophysics*, *79*(8), 2510–2522.

Boduroglu, A., & Shah, P. (2014). Configural representations in spatial working memory. *Visual Cognition*, *22*(1), 102–124.

Brady, T. F., & Alvarez, G. A. (2010). Ensemble statistics of a display influence the representation of items in visual working memory. *Visual Cognition*, *18*(1), 114–118.

Brady, T. F., & Alvarez, G. A. (2011). Hierarchical encoding in visual working memory: Ensemble statistics bias memory for individual items. *Psychological Science*, *22*(3), 384–392.

Brady, T. F., & Alvarez, G. A. (2015a). No evidence for a fixed object limit in working memory: Spatial ensemble representations inflate estimates of working memory capacity for complex objects. *Journal of Experimental Psychology: Learning, Memory, and Cognition*, *41*(3), 921.

Brady, T. F., & Alvarez, G. A. (2015b). Contextual effects in visual working memory reveal hierarchically structured memory representations. *Journal of Vision*, *15*(15), 6–6.

Brady, T. F., Konkle, T., & Alvarez, G. A. (2009). Compression in visual working memory: Using statistical regularities to form more efficient memory representations. *Journal of Experimental Psychology: General*, *138*(4), 487–502.

Brand, J., Oriet, C., & Sykes Tottenham, L. (2012). Size and emotion averaging: Costs of dividing attention after all. *Canadian Journal of Experimental Psychology/Revue Canadienne De Psychologie Expérimentale*, *66*(1), 63.

Brezis, N., Bronfman, Z., & Usher, M. (2015). Adaptive spontaneous transitions between two mechanisms of numerical averaging. *Scientific Reports*, *5*, 10415.

Brezis, N., Bronfman, Z. Z., & Usher, M. (2018). A perceptual-like population-coding mechanism of approximate numerical averaging. *Neural Computation*, *30*(2), 428–446.

Brezis, N., Bronfman, Z. Z., Jacoby, N., Lavidor, M., & Usher, M. (2016). Transcranial direct current stimulation over the parietal cortex improves approximate numerical averaging. *Journal of Cognitive Neuroscience*, *28*(11), 1700–1713.

Bronfman, Z. Z., Brezis, N., Jacobson, H., & Usher, M. (2014). We see more than we can report: "Cost free" color phenomenality outside focal attention. *Psychological Science*, *25*(7), 1394–1403.

Burr, D., & Ross, J. (2008). A visual sense of number. *Current Biology, 18*(6), 425–428.

Campbell, F. W., & Robson, J. G. (1968). Application of Fourier analysis to the visibility of gratings. *The Journal of Physiology, 197*(3), 551–566.

Cant J. S., & Xu Y. (2012). Object ensemble processing in human anterior-medial ventral visual cortex. *Journal of Neuroscience, 32*, 7685–7700.

Cant, J. S., & Xu, Y. (2015). The impact of density and ratio on object-ensemble representation in human anterior-medial ventral visual cortex. *Cerebral Cortex, 25*(11), 4226–4239.

Cant, J. S., & Xu, Y. (2017). The contribution of object shape and surface properties to object ensemble representation in anterior-medial ventral visual cortex. *Journal of Cognitive Neuroscience, 29*(2), 398–412.

Cant, J. S., Sun, S. Z., & Xu, Y. (2015). Distinct cognitive mechanisms involved in the processing of single objects and object ensembles. *Journal of Vision, 15*(4), 12–12.

Cha, O., & Chong, S. C. (2018). Perceived average orientation reflects effective gist of the surface. *Psychological Science, 29*(3), 319–327.

Cha, O., Blake, R., & Chong, S. C. (2018). Composite binocular perception from dichoptic stimulus arrays with similar ensemble information. *Scientific Reports, 8*, 8263.

Cha, O., Blake, R., & Gauthier, I. (2022). Contribution of a common ability in average and variability judgments. *Psychonomic Bulletin & Review, 29*(1), 108–115.

Chang, T.-Y., & Gauthier, I. (2021). Domain-general ability underlies complex object ensemble processing. *Journal of Experimental Psychology: General. 151*(4), 966–972

Chen, B., & Zhou, G. (2018). Attentional modulation of hierarchical ensemble coding for the identities of moving faces. *Journal of Experimental Psychology: Human Perception and Performance, 44*(10), 1542–1556.

Chetverikov, A., Campana, G., & Kristjánsson, Á. (2016). Building ensemble representations: How the shape of preceding distractor distributions affects visual search. *Cognition, 153*, 196–210.

Chetverikov, A., Campana, G., & Kristjansson, A. (2017a). Rapid learning of visual ensembles. *Journal of Vision, 17*(2), 21, 1–15.

Chetverikov, A., Campana, G., & Kristjánsson, Á. (2017b). Representing color ensembles. *Psychological Science, 28*(10), 1510–1517.

Chetverikov, A., Campana, G., & Kristjánsson, Á. (2017c). Set size manipulations reveal the boundary conditions of perceptual ensemble learning. *Vision Research, 140*, 144–156.

Chetverikov, A., Hansmann-Roth, S., Tanrikulu, Ö. D., & Kristjansson, Á. (2019). Feature distribution learning (FDL): A new method for studying visual ensembles perception with priming of attention shifts. In *Spatial learning and attention guidance* (ed. Wolfgang Walz) (pp. 37–57). Humana, New York.

Cho, J., & Chong, S. C. (2019). Search termination when the target is absent: The prevalence of coarse processing and its intertrial influence. *Journal of Experimental Psychology: Human Perception and Performance, 45*(11), 1455–1469.

Choi, Y. M., & Chong, S. C. (2020). Effects of selective attention on mean-size computation: Weighted averaging and perceptual enlargement. *Psychological Science, 31*(10), 1261–1271.

Chong, S. C., & Evans, K. K. (2011). Distributed versus focused attention (count vs estimate). *Wiley Interdisciplinary Reviews: Cognitive Science, 2*(6), 634–638.

Chong, S. C., & Treisman, A. (2003). Representation of statistical properties. *Vision Research, 43*, 393–404.

Chong, S. C., & Treisman, A. (2005a). Attentional spread in the statistical processing of visual displays. *Perception & Psychophysics, 67*(1), 1–13.

Chong, S. C., & Treisman, A. (2005b). Statistical processing: Computing the average size in perceptual groups. *Vision Research*, *45*, 891–900

Chong, S. C., Joo, S. J., Emmanouil, T.-A., & Treisman, A. (2008). Statistical processing: not so implausible after all. *Perception & Psychophysics*, *70*(7), 1327–1334.

Choo, H., & Franconeri, S. L. (2010). Objects with reduced visibility still contribute to size averaging. *Attention, Perception, & Psychophysics*, *72*(1), 86–99.

Cohen, M. A., & Chun, M. M. (2017). Studying consciousness through inattentional blindness, change blindness, and the attentional blink. In *The Blackwell Companion to Consciousness* (eds S. Schneider & M. Velmans) (pp. 539–550). John Wiley & Sons, New York.

Cohen, M. A., Dennett, D. C., & Kanwisher, N. (2016). What is the bandwidth of perceptual experience? *Trends in Cognitive Sciences*, 20(5), 324–335.

Cooper, E. A., & Radonjić, A. (2016). Gender representation in the vision sciences: A longitudinal study. *Journal of Vision*, *16*(1), 1–10.

Corbett, J. E. (2017). The whole warps the sum of its parts: Gestalt-defined-group mean size biases memory for individual objects. *Psychological Science*, *28*(1), 12–22.

Corbett, J. E., Greenwood, J., & Munneke, J. (osf.io/e3dvq/) Smart perception? Gestalt grouping, perceptual averaging, and memory capacity.

Corbett, J. E., & Melcher, D. (2014a). Characterizing ensemble statistics: Mean size is represented across multiple frames of reference. *Attention, Perception, & Psychophysics*, *76*(3), 746–758.

Corbett, J. E., & Melcher, D. (2014b). Stable statistical representations facilitate visual search. *Journal of Experimental Psychology: Human Perception and Performance*, *40*(5), 1915.

Corbett, J. E., & Munneke, J. (2018). "It's not a tumor": A framework for capitalizing on individual diversity to boost target detection. *Psychological Science*, *29*(10), 1692–1705.

Corbett, J. E., & Munneke, J. (2020). Statistical stability and set size exert distinct influences on visual search. *Attention, Perception, & Psychophysics, 40 Years of Feature Integration: Special Issue in Memory of Anne Treisman*, *82*(*2*), 832–839.

Corbett, J. E., & Oriet, C. (2011). The whole is indeed more than the sum of its parts: Perceptual averaging in the absence of individual item representation. *Acta Psychologica*, *138*(2), 289–301.

Corbett, J. E., Fischer, J., & Whitney, D. (2011). Facilitating stable representations: Serial dependence in vision. *PLoS One*, *6*(1), e16701.

Corbett, J. E., Oriet, C., & Rensink, R. A. (2006). The rapid extraction of numeric meaning. *Vision Research*, *46*(10), 1559–1573.

Corbett, J. E., Venuti, P., & Melcher, D. (2016). Perceptual averaging in individuals with autism spectrum disorder. *Frontiers in Psychology, 7,* 1735.

Corbett, J. E., Wurnitsch, N., Schwartz, A., & Whitney, D. (2012). An aftereffect of adaptation to mean size. *Visual Cognition, 20*(2), 211–231.

Corbett, J. E., & Song, J.-H. (2014). Statistical extraction affects visually guided action. *Visual Cognition, 22*(7), 881–895.

Corbett, J. E., Aydın, B., & Munneke, J. (2021). Adaptation to average duration. *Attention, Perception, & Psychophysics, 83,* 1190–1200.

Cowan, N. (2001). The magical number 4 in short-term memory: A reconsideration of mental storage capacity. *Behavioral and Brain Sciences, 24*(1), 87–114.

Crawford, L. E., Corbin, J. C., & Landy, D. (2019). Prior experience informs ensemble encoding. *Psychonomic Bulletin & Review, 26*(3), 993–1000.

Cui, L., & Liu, Z. (2021). Synergy between research on ensemble perception, data visualization, and statistics education: A tutorial review. *Attention, Perception, & Psychophysics, 83*(3), 1290–1311.

Dakin, S. C. (2001). Information limit on the spatial integration of local orientation signals. *JOSA A, 18*(5), 1016–1026.

Dakin, S. C., Bex, P. J., Cass, J. R., & Watt, R. J. (2009). Dissociable effects of attention and crowding on orientation averaging. *Journal of Vision, 9*(11), 1–16.

Dakin, S. C., Mareschal, I., & Bex, P. J. (2005). Local and global limitations on direction integration assessed using equivalent noise analysis. *Vision research, 45*(24), 3027–3049.

Dakin, S. C., & Watt, R. J. (1997). The computation of orientation statistics from visual texture. *Vision Research, 37*(22), 3181–3192.

De Fockert, J. W., & Marchant, A. P. (2008). Attention modulates set representation by statistical properties. *Perception & Psychophysics, 70*(5), 789–794.

De Fockert, J., & Wolfenstein, C. (2009). Short article: Rapid extraction of mean identity from sets of faces. *Quarterly Journal of Experimental Psychology, 62*(9), 1716–1722.

De Gardelle, V., & Summerfield, C. (2011). Robust averaging during perceptual judgment. *Proceedings of the National Academy of Sciences, 108*(32), 13341–13346.

de Haan, B., Karnath, H. O., & Driver, J. (2012). Mechanisms and anatomy of unilateral extinction after brain injury. *Neuropsychologia, 50*(6), 1045–1053.

Deese, J. (1959). On the prediction of occurrence of particular verbal intrusions in immediate recall. *Journal of Experimental Psychology, 58*(1), 17–22.

Demeyere, N., Rzeskiewicz, A., Humphreys, K. A., & Humphreys, G. W. (2008). Automatic statistical processing of visual properties in simultanagnosia. Neuropsychologia, 46(11), 2861–2864.

Dodgson, D. B., & Raymond, J. E. (2020). Value associations bias ensemble perception. *Attention, Perception, & Psychophysics*, *82*(1), 109–117.

Driver, J., & Vuilleumier, P. (2001). Perceptual awareness and its loss in unilateral neglect and extinction. *Cognition*, *79*(1–2), 39–88.

Dubé, C., & Sekuler, R. (2015). Obligatory and adaptive averaging in visual short-term memory. *Journal of Vision*, *15*(4), 1–13.

Durgin, F. H. (1995). Texture density adaptation and the perceived numerosity and distribution of texture. *Journal of Experimental Psychology: Human Perception and Performance*, *21*(1), 149–169.

Durgin, F. H. (2008). Texture density adaptation and visual number revisited. *Current Biology*, *18*(18), R855–R856.

Durgin, F. H., & Huk, A. C. (1997). Texture density aftereffects in the perception of artificial and natural textures. *Vision research*, *37*(23), 3273–3282.

Durgin, F. H., & Proffitt, D. R. (1996). Visual learning in the perception of texture: simple and contingent aftereffects of texture density. *Spatial Vision*, *9*(4), 423.

Emmanouil, T. A., & Treisman, A. (2008). Dividing attention across feature dimensions in statistical processing of perceptual groups. *Perception & Psychophysics*, *70*(6), 946–954.

Epstein, M. L., & Emmanouil, T. A. (2017). Ensemble coding remains accurate under object and spatial visual working memory load. *Attention, Perception, & Psychophysics*, *79*(7), 2088–2097.

Epstein, M. L., & Emmanouil, T. A. (2021). Ensemble statistics can be available before individual item properties: Electroencephalography evidence using the Oddball paradigm. *Journal of Cognitive Neuroscience*, *33*(6), 1056–1068.

Epstein, M. L., Quilty-Dunn, J., Mandelbaum, E., & Emmanouil, T. A. (2020). The outlier paradox: The role of iterative ensemble coding in discounting outliers. *Journal of Experimental Psychology: Human Perception and Performance*, *46*(11), 1267–1279.

Fan, A. W.-Y., Guo, L. L., Frost, A. et al. (2021). Grasping of real-world objects is not biased by ensemble perception. *Frontiers in Psychology*, *12*, 597691.

Fischer, J., & Whitney, D. (2011). Object-level visual information gets through the bottleneck of crowding. *Journal of Neurophysiology*, *106*(3), 1389–1398.

Fouriezos, G., Rubenfeld, S., & Capstick, G. (2008). Visual statistical decisions. *Perception & Psychophysics*, *70*(3), 456–464.

Galton, F. (1907). Vox populi (the wisdom of crowds). *Nature*, *75*(7), 450–451.

Georgopoulos, A. P., Schwartz, A. B., & Kettner, R. E. (1986). Neuronal population coding of movement direction. *Science*, *233*(4771), 1416–1419.

Gillen C., & Heath M. (2014a). Perceptual averaging governs antisaccade endpoint bias. *Experimental Brain Research*, 232 (10), 3201–3210.

Gillen C., & Heath M. (2014b). Target frequency influences antisaccade endpoint bias: Evidence for perceptual averaging. *Vision Research*, 105, 151–158.

Goldenberg, A., Weisz, E., Sweeny, T. D., Cikara, M., & Gross, J. J. (2021). The crowd-emotion-amplification effect. *Psychological Science*, *32*(3), 437–450.

Haberman, J., Brady, T. F., & Alvarez, G. A. (2015). Individual differences in ensemble perception reveal multiple, independent levels of ensemble representation. *Journal of Experimental Psychology: General*, *144*(2), 432.

Haberman, J., Harp, T., & Whitney, D. (2009). Averaging facial expression over time. *Journal of Vision*, *9*(11), 1–13.

Haberman, J., Lee, P., & Whitney, D. (2015). Mixed emotions: Sensitivity to facial variance in a crowd of faces. *Journal of Vision*, *15*(4), 16.

Halberda, J., Sires, S. F., & Feigenson, L. (2006). Multiple spatially overlapping sets can be enumerated in parallel. *Psychological Science*, *17*(7), 572–576.

Haberman, J., & Suresh, S. (2021). Ensemble size judgments account for size constancy. *Attention, Perception, & Psychophysics*, *83*(3), 925–933.

Haberman, J., & Whitney, D. (2007). Rapid extraction of mean emotion and gender from sets of faces. *Current Biology*, *17*, R751–R753.

Haberman, J., & Whitney, D. (2009). Seeing the mean: Ensemble coding for sets of faces. *Journal of Experimental Psychology: Human Perception and Performance*, *35*, 718–734.

Haberman, J., & Whitney, D. (2010). The visual system discounts emotional deviants when extracting average expression. *Attention, Perception, & Psychophysics*, *72*(7), 1825–1838.

Haberman, J., & Whitney, D. (2012). Ensemble perception: Summarizing the scene and broadening the limits of visual processing. *From perception to consciousness: Searching with Anne Treisman*, 339–349.

Hamidi, M., Giuffre, L., & Heath, M. (2021). A summary statistical representation influences perceptions but not visually or memory-guided grasping. *Human Movement Science*, *75*, 102739.

Hansmann-Roth, S., Kristjánsson, Á., Whitney, D., & Chetverikov, A. (2021). Dissociating implicit and explicit ensemble representations reveals the limits of visual perception and the richness of behavior. *Scientific Reports*, *11*(1), 1–12.

Happé, F., & Frith, U. (2006). The weak coherence account: detail-focused cognitive style in autism spectrum disorders. *Journal of autism and developmental disorders*, *36*(1), 5–25.

Harrison, W. J., McMaster, J. M., & Bays, P. M. (2021). Limited memory for ensemble statistics in visual change detection. *Cognition*, *214*, 104763.

Harrison, L., Yang, F., Franconeri, S., & Chang, R. (2014). Ranking visualizations of correlation using weber's law. *IEEE Transactions on Visualization and Computer Graphics*, *20*(12), 1943–1952.

Hochstein, S. (2016). The power of populations: How the brain represents features and summary statistics. *Journal of Vision*, 16(12), 1117.

Hochstein, S. (2020). The gist of Anne Treisman's revolution. *Attention, Perception, & Psychophysics*, *82*(1), 24–30.

Hochstein, S., & Ahissar, M. (2002). View from the top: Hierarchies and reverse hierarchies in the visual system. *Neuron*, *36*(5), 791–804.

Hochstein, S., & Pavlovskaya, M. (2020). Perceptual learning of ensemble and outlier perception. *Journal of Vision*, *20*(8), 13, 1–17.

Hochstein, S., Pavlovskaya, M., Bonneh, Y. S., & Soroker, N. (2015). Global statistics are not neglected. *Journal of Vision*, *15*(4), 7.

Hochstein, S., Pavlovskaya, M., Bonneh, Y. S., & Soroker, N. (2018). Comparing set summary statistics and outlier pop out in vision. *Journal of Vision*, *18*(13), 12.

Hollingworth, H. L. (1910). The central tendency of judgment. *The Journal of Philosophy, Psychology and Scientific Methods*, *7*(17), 461–469.

Holway, A. H., & Boring, E. G. (1941). Determinants of apparent visual size with distance variant. *The American Journal of Psychology*, *54*(1), 21–37.

Hommel, B., & Akyürek, E. G. (2005). Lag-1 sparing in the attentional blink: Benefits and costs of integrating two events into a single episode. *Quarterly Journal of Experimental Psychology*, 58A, 1415–1433.

Huang, L. (2015). Statistical properties demand as much attention as object features. *PLoS One*, *10*(8), e0131191.

Hubel, D. H., & Wiesel, T. N. (1959). Receptive fields of single neurones in the cat's striate cortex. *The Journal of Physiology*, *148*(3), 574–591.

Hubel, D. H., & Wiesel, T. N. (1962). Receptive fields, binocular interaction and functional architecture in the cat's visual cortex. *The Journal of Physiology*, *160*(1), 106–154.

Hubert-Wallander, B., & Boynton, G. M. (2015). Not all summary statistics are made equal: Evidence from extracting summaries across time. *Journal of Vision*, *15*(4), 1–12.

Iakovlev, A. U., & Utochkin, I. S. (2021). Roles of saliency and set size in ensemble averaging. *Attention, Perception, & Psychophysics*, *83*(3), 1251–1262.

Im, H. Y., & Chong, S. C. (2009). Computation of mean size is based on perceived size. *Attention, Perception, & Psychophysics*, *71*(2), 375–384.

Im, H. Y., & Chong, S. C. (2014). Mean size as a unit of visual working memory. *Perception*, *43*(7), 663–676.

Im, H. Y., Chong, S. C., Sun, J. et al. (2017). Cross-cultural and hemispheric laterality effects on the ensemble coding of emotion in facial crowds. *Culture & Brain*, 5, 125–152.

Im, H. Y., Cushing, C. A., Ward, N., & Kveraga, K. (2021). Differential neurodynamics and connectivity in the dorsal and ventral visual pathways during perception of emotional crowds and individuals: a MEG study. *Cognitive, Affective, & Behavioral Neuroscience*, *21*(4), 776–792.

Im, H. Y., & Halberda, J. (2013). The effects of sampling and internal noise on the representation of ensemble average size. *Attention, Perception, & Psychophysics*, *75*(2), 278–286.

Im, H. Y., Park, W. J., & Chong, S. C. (2015). Ensemble statistics as units of selection. *Journal of Cognitive Psychology*, *27*(1), 114–127.

Im, H. Y., Tiurina, N. A., & Utochkin, I. S. (2021). An explicit investigation of the roles that feature distributions play in rapid visual categorization. *Attention, Perception, and Psychophysics*, *83*, 1050–1069.

Jackson-Nielsen, M., Cohen, M. A., & Pitts, M. A. (2017). Perception of ensemble statistics requires attention. *Consciousness and Cognition*, *48*, 149–160.

Jacoby, O., Kamke, M. R., & Mattingley, J. B. (2013). Is the whole really more than the sum of its parts? Estimates of average size and orientation are susceptible to object substitution masking. *Journal of Experimental Psychology: Human Perception and Performance*, *39*(1), 233–244.

Jeong, J., & Chong, S. C. (2020). Adaptation to mean and variance: Interrelationships between mean and variance representations in orientation perception. *Vision Research*, *167*, 46–53.

Ji, L., Chen, W., & Fu, X. (2014, June). Different roles of foveal and extrafoveal vision in ensemble representation for facial expressions. In *International Conference on Engineering Psychology and Cognitive Ergonomics* (ed. D. Harris) (pp. 164–173). Springer, Cham.

Ji, L., & Pourtois, G. (2018). Capacity limitations to extract the mean emotion from multiple facial expressions depend on emotion variance. *Vision Research*, *145*, 39–48.

Johnston, A., Arnold, D. H., & Nishida, S. (2006). Spatially localized distortions of event time. *Current Biology*, *16*(5), 472–479.

Joo, S. J., Shin, K., Chong, S. C., & Blake, R. (2009). On the nature of the stimulus information necessary for estimating mean size of visual arrays. *Journal of Vision*, *9*(9), 7.

Jung, W., Bülthoff, I., & Armann, R. G. (2017). The contribution of foveal and peripheral visual information to ensemble representation of face race. *Journal of Vision*, *17*(13), 11.

Kacin, M., Gauthier, I., & Cha, O. (2021). Ensemble coding of average length and average orientation are correlated. *Vision Research*, *187*, 94–181.

Kahneman, D. (2011). *Thinking, fast and slow*. Macmillan.

Kanaya, S., Hayashi, M. J., & Whitney, D. (2018). Exaggerated groups: Amplification in ensemble coding of temporal and spatial features. *Proceedings of the Royal Society B- Biological Sciences*, *285*(20172770), 1–9.

Karaminis, T., Neil, L., Manning, C. et al. (2017). Ensemble perception of emotions in children with autism is similar to typically developing children. *Developmental Cognitive Neuroscience*, *24*, 51–62.

Khayat, N., Fusi, S., & Hochstein, S. (2021). Perceiving ensemble statistics of novel image sets. *Attention, Perception, & Psychophysics*, *83*, 1312–1328.

Khayat, N., & Hochstein, S. (2018). Perceiving set mean and range: Automaticity and precision. *Journal of Vision*, *18*(9), 23.

Khayat, N., & Hochstein, S. (2019). Relating categorization to set summary statistics perception. *Attention, Perception, & Psychophys*ics, *81*, 2850–2872.

Khvostov, V. A., Lukashevich, A. O., & Utochkin, I. S. (2021). Spatially intermixed objects of different categories are parsed automatically. *Scientific Reports*, *11*(377), 1–8.

Khvostov, V. A., & Utochkin, I. S. (2019). Independent and parallel visual processing of ensemble statistics: Evidence from dual tasks. *Journal of Vision*, *19*(9), 3.

Kim, M., & Chong, S. C. (2020). The visual system does not compute a single mean but summarizes a distribution. *Journal of Experimental Psychology: Human Perception and Performance*, *46*(9), 1013–1028.

Kramer, R. S. S., Ritchie, K. L., & Burton, A. M. (2015). Viewers extract the mean from images of the same person: A route to face learning. *Journal of Vision*, *15*(4), 1, 1–9.

Lanzoni, L., Melcher, D., Miceli, G., & Corbett, J. E. (2014). Global statistical regularities modulate the speed of visual search in patients with focal attentional deficits. *"Zooming in on the Big Picture: Current Issues in Global versus Local Processing," Special Issue Frontiers in Psychology, Perception Science*, *5*(a514), 12.

Lau, J. S. H., & Brady, T. F. (2018). Ensemble statistics accessed through proxies: Range heuristic and dependence on low-level properties in variability discrimination. *Journal of Vision*, *18*(9), 3.

Lee, H., Baek, J., & Chong, S. C. (2016). Perceived magnitude of visual displays: Area, numerosity, and mean size. *Journal of Vision*, *16*(3), 12.

Lew, T. F., & Vul, E. (2013): Environment sensitivity in hierarchical representations. *Visual Cognition*, *21*(6), 693–697.

Lew, T. F., & Vul, E. (2015). Ensemble clustering in visual working memory biases location memories and reduces the Weber noise of relative positions. *Journal of Vision*, *15*(4), 10, 1–14.

Li, F. F., VanRullen, R., Koch, C., & Perona, P. (2002). Rapid natural scene categorization in the near absence of attention. *Proceedings of the National Academy of Sciences*, *99*(14), 9596–9601.

Li, H., Ji, L., Tong, K. et al. (2016). Processing of individual items during ensemble coding of facial expressions. *Frontiers in Psychology*, *7*, 1332.

Li, K. A., & Yeh, S. L. (2017). Mean size estimation yields left-side bias: role of attention on perceptual averaging. *Attention, Perception, & Psychophysics*, *79*(8), 2538–2551.

Li, V., Herce Castañón, S., Solomon, J. A., Vandormael, H., & Summerfield, C. (2017). Robust averaging protects decisions from noise in neural computations. *PLoS Computational Biology*, *13*(8), e1005723.

Lowe, M. X., Stevenson, R. A., Barense, M. D., Cant, J. S., & Ferber, S. (2018). Relating the perception of visual ensemble statistics to individual levels of autistic traits. *Attention, Perception, & Psychophysics*, *80*(7), 1667–1674.

Luck, S. J., & Vogel, E. K. (1997). The capacity of visual working memory for features and conjunctions. *Nature*, *390*(6657), 279–281.

Luo, A. X., & Zhao, J. (2018). Capacity limit of ensemble perception of multiple spatially intermixed sets. *Attention, Perception, & Psychophysics*, *80*(8), 2033–2047.

Ma, W. J., Beck, J. M., Latham, P. E., & Pouget, A. (2006). Bayesian inference with probabilistic population codes. *Nature Neuroscience*, *9*(11), 1432–1438.

Malpass, R. S., & Kravitz, J. (1969). Recognition for faces of own and other race. *Journal of Personality and Social Psychology*, 13, 330–335.

Manassi, M., Ghirardo, C., Canas-Bajo, T. et al. (2021). Serial dependence in the perceptual judgments of radiologists. *Cognitive Research: Principles and Implications*, *6*(1), 65.

Manassi, M., Liberman, A., Chaney, W., & Whitney, D. (2017). The perceived stability of scenes: serial dependence in ensemble representations. *Scientific Reports*, 7(1), 1–9.

Marchant A. P., Simons D. J., & de Fockert J. W. (2013). Ensemble representations: Effects of set size and item heterogeneity on average size perception. *Acta Psychologica*, *142*(2), 245–250.

Markov, Y., & Tiurina, N. (2021). Size-distance rescaling in the ensemble representation of range: Study with binocular and monocular cues. *Acta Psychologica*, *213*, 103238.

Markov, Y., Tiurina, N. A., Stakina, Y., & Utochkin, I. S. (2017). The capacity and precision of visual working memory for objects and ensembles. *Psychology*, *14*(4), 735–755.

Maule, J., & Franklin, A. (2015). Effects of ensemble complexity and perceptual similarity on rapid averaging of hue. *Journal of Vision*, *15*(4), 6.

Maule, J., & Franklin, A. (2016) Accurate rapid averaging of multihue ensembles is due to a limited capacity subsampling. *Journal of the Optical Society of America A*, 33(3), A22–A29.

Maule, J., & Franklin, A. (2020). Adaptation to variance generalizes across visual domains. *Journal of Experimental Psychology: General, 149*(4), 662–675.

Maule, J., Stanworth, K., Pellicano, E., & Franklin, A. (2017). Ensemble perception of color in autistic adults. *Autism Research, 10*(5), 839–851.

Maule, J., Witzel, C., & Franklin, A. (2014). Getting the gist of multiple hues: metric and categorical effects on ensemble perception of hue. *Journal of the Optical Society of America, 31*(4), A93–A102.

McDermott, J. H., Schemitsch, M., & Simoncelli, E. P. (2013). Summary statistics in auditory perception. *Nature Neuroscience, 16*(4), 493–500.

McNair, N. A., Goodbourn, P. T., Shone, L. T., & Harris, I. M. (2017). Summary statistics in the attentional blink. *Attention, Perception, & Psychophysics, 79*(*1*), 100–116.

Messenger, J. F. (1903). The perception of number. *The Psychological Review: Monograph Supplements, 5*(5), i–44.

Michael E., de Gardelle V., & Summerfield C. (2014). Priming by the variability of visual information. *Proceedings of the National Academy of Sciences, 111*(21), 7873–7878.

Miller, A., Pedersen, V., & Sheldon, R. (1970). Magnitude estimation of average length: A follow-up. *The American Journal of Psychology, 83*(1), 95–102.

Miller, A. L., & Sheldon, R. (1969). Magnitude estimation of average length and average inclination. *Journal of Experimental Psychology, 81*(1), 16–21.

Moerel, D., Ling, S., & Jehee, J. F. (2016). Perceptual learning increases orientation sampling efficiency. *Journal of Vision, 16*(3), 1–9.

Moore, C. M., & Egeth, H. (1997). Perception without attention: Evidence of grouping under conditions of inattention. *Journal of Experimental Psychology: Human Perception and Performance*, 23(2), 339–352.

Morgan, M., Chubb, C., & Solomon, J. A. (2008). A 'dipper' function for texture discrimination based on orientation variance. *Journal of Vision, 8*(11), 9.

Munneke, J., Duymaz, İ., & Corbett, J. E. (2022). Value-driven effects on perceptual averaging. *Attention, Perception, & Psychophysics, 84*(3), 781–794.

Myczek, K., & Simons, D. J. (2008). Better than average: Alternatives to statistical summary representations for rapid judgments of average size. *Perception & Psychophysics, 70*(5), 772–788.

Neumann, M. F., Schweinberger, S. R., & Burton, A. M. (2013). Viewers extract mean and individual identity from sets of famous faces. *Cognition, 128*(1), 56–63.

Norman, L. J., Heywood, C. A., & Kentridge, R. W. (2015). Direct encoding of orientation variance in the visual system. *Journal of Vision, 15*(4), 3.

Olkkonen, M., McCarthy, P. F., & Allred, S. R. (2014). The central tendency bias in color perception: Effects of internal and external noise. *Journal of Vision, 14* (11), 5, 1–15.

Oriet, C., & Brand, J. (2013). Size averaging of irrelevant stimuli cannot be prevented. *Vision Research, 79*, 8–16.

Oriet, C., & Hozempa, K. (2016). Incidental statistical summary representation over time. *Journal of Vision, 16*, 3, 1–14.

Pardilla-Delgado, E., & Payne, J. D. (2017). The Deese-Roediger-McDermott (DRM) task: A simple cognitive paradigm to investigate false memories in the laboratory. *Journal of visualized experiments: JoVE,* (119), e54793.

Park, J., & Park, S. (2017). Conjoint representation of texture ensemble and location in the parahippocampal place area. *Journal of Neurophysiology, 117*(4), 1595–1607.

Parkes, L., Lund, J., Angelucci, A., Solomon, J. A., & Morgan, M. (2001). Compulsory averaging of crowded orientation signals in human vision. *Nature Neuroscience, 4*(7), 739–744.

Pascucci, D., Ruethemann, N., & Plomp, G. (2021). The anisotropic field of ensemble coding. *Scientific Reports, 11*(1), 1–10.

Pavlovskaya, M., & Hochstein, S. (2011). Perceptual learning transfer between hemispheres and tasks for easy and hard feature search conditions. *Journal of Vision, 11*(1), 8.

Pavlovskaya, M., Ring, H., Groswasser, Z., & Hochstein, S. (2002). Searching with unilateral neglect. *Journal of Cognitive Neuroscience, 14*(5), 745–756.

Pavlovskaya, M., Soroker, N., Bonneh, Y. S., & Hochstein, S. (2015). Computing an average when part of the population is not perceived. *Journal of Cognitive Neuroscience, 27*(7), 1397–1411.

Peng, S., Liu, C. H., Yang, X. et al. (2020). Culture variation in the average identity extraction: The role of global vs. local processing orientation. *Visual Cognition, 28*(3), 180–191.

Piazza, E. A., Sweeny, T. D., Wessel, D., Silver, M. A., & Whitney, D. (2013). Humans use summary statistics to perceive auditory sequences. *Psychological Science, 24*(8), 1389–1397.

Poltoratski, S., & Xu, Y. (2013). The association of color memory and the enumeration of multiple spatially overlapping sets. *Journal of vision, 13*(8), 1–11.

Potter, M. C., & Faulconer, B. A. (1975). Time to understand pictures and words. *Nature, 253*(5491), 437–438.

Prasad, D., & Bainbridge, W. A. (2021). The visual Mandela effect: Evidence for specific shared false memories in popular iconography. *Journal of Vision, 21*(9), 2121–2121.

Raidvee, A., Toom, M., Averin, K., & Aliik, J. (2020). Perception of means, sums, and areas. *Attention, Perception and Psychophysics, 82*(2), 865–876.

Raymond, J. E., Shapiro, K. L., & Arnell, K. M. (1992). Temporary suppression of visual processing in an RSVP task: An attentional blink?. *Journal of Experimental Psychology: Human Perception and Performance, 18*(3), 849–860.

Rensink, R. A. (2004). Visual sensing without seeing. *Psychological Science, 15*(1), 27–32.

Rensink, R. A. (2017). The nature of correlation perception in scatterplots. *Psychonomic Bulletin & Review, 24*(3), 776–797.

Rensink, R. A., & Baldridge, G. (2010, June). The perception of correlation in scatterplots. In *Computer Graphics Forum* (eds G. Melançon, T. Munzner, and D. Weiskopf) (Vol. 29, No. 3, pp. 1203–1210). Oxford: Blackwell.

Rensink, R. A., O'regan, J. K., & Clark, J. J. (1997). To see or not to see: The need for attention to perceive changes in scenes. *Psychological Science, 8*(5), 368–373.

Rhodes, G., Neumann, M. F., Ewing, L., & Palermo, R. (2015). Reduced set averaging of face identity in children and adolescents with autism. *Quarterly Journal of Experimental Psychology, 68*(7), 1391–1403.

Robitaille, N., & Harris, I. M. (2011). When more is less: Extraction of summary statistics benefits from larger sets. *Journal of Vision, 11*(12), 1–8.

Roediger, H. L., & McDermott, K. B. (1995). Creating false memories: Remembering words not presented in lists. *Journal of experimental psychology: Learning, Memory, and Cognition, 21*(4), 803–814.

Rosenholtz, R. (2001). Visual search for orientation among heterogeneous distractors: Experimental results and implications for signal-detection theory models of search. *Journal of Experimental Psychology: Human Perception and Performance, 27*(4), 985–999.

Sama, M. A., Srikanthan, D., Nestor, A., & Cant, J. S. (2021). Global and local interference effects in ensemble encoding are best explained by interactions between summary representations of the mean and the range. *Attention, Perception, & Psychophysics, 83*(3), 1106–1128.

Schweickert, R., Han, H. J., Yamaguchi, M., & Fortin, C. (2014). Estimating averages from distributions of tone durations. *Attention, Perception, & Psychophysics, 76*(2), 605–620.

Semizer, Y., & Boduroglu, A. (2021). Variability leads to overestimation of mean summaries. *Attention, Perception, & Psychophysics*, *83*(3), 1129–1140.

Solomon, J. A. (2009). The history of dipper functions. *Attention, Perception, & Psychophysics*, *71*(3), 435–443.

Solomon, J. A. (2010). Visual discrimination of orientation statistics in crowded and uncrowded arrays. *Journal of Vision*, *10*(14), 19.

Solomon, J. A., & Morgan, M. J. (2017) Orientation-defined boundaries are detected with low efficiency. *Vision Research* 138, 66–70.

Solomon, J. A., & Morgan, M. J. (2018). Calculation efficiencies for mean numerosity. *Psychological Science*, *29*(11), 1824–1831.

Solomon, J. A., Morgan, M., & Chubb, C. (2011). Efficiencies for the statistics of size discrimination. *Journal of Vision*, *11*(12), 13.

Son, G., Oh, B.-I., Kang, M.-S., & Chong, S. C. (2020). Similarity-based clusters are representational units of visual working memory. *Journal of Experimental Psychology: Learning, Memory, and Cognition*, *46*(1), 46–59.

Sun, J., & Chong, S. C. (2020). Power of averaging: Noise reduction by ensemble coding of multiple faces. *Journal of Experimental Psychology: General*, *149*(3), 550–563.

Sweeny, T. D., Haroz, S., & Whitney, D. (2013). Perceiving group behavior: Sensitive ensemble coding mechanisms for biological motion of human crowds. *Journal of Experimental Psychology: Human Perception and Performance*, *39*(2), 329–337.

Sweeny, T. D., & Whitney, D. (2014). Perceiving crowd attention ensemble perception of a crowd's gaze. *Psychological Science*, *25*(10), 1903–1913.

Sweeny, T. D., Wurnitsch, N., Gopnik, A., & Whitney, D. (2015). Ensemble perception of size in 4–5-year-old children. *Developmental science*, *18*(4), 556–568.

Szafir, D. A., Haroz, S., Gleicher, M., & Franconeri, S. (2016). Four types of ensemble coding in data visualizations. *Journal of Vision*, *16*(5), 11.

Takano, Y., & Kimura, E. (2020). Task-driven and flexible mean judgment for heterogeneous luminance ensembles. *Attention, Perception & Psychophysics*, *82*(2), 877–890.

Tark, K. J., Kang, M. S., Chong, S. C., & Shim, W. M. (2021). Neural representations of ensemble coding in the occipital and parietal cortices. *NeuroImage*, *245*, 118680.

Thorpe, S., Fize, D., & Marlot, C. (1996). Speed of processing in the human visual system. *Nature*, *381*(6582), 520–522.

Tiurina, N. A., & Utochkin, I. S. (2019). Ensemble perception in depth: Correct size-distance rescaling of multiple objects before averaging. *Journal of Experimental Psychology: General*, *148*(4), 728–738.

Tokita, M., Ueda, S., & Ishiguchi, A. (2016). Evidence for a global sampling process in extraction of summary statistics of item sizes in a set. *Frontiers in Psychology*, *7*, 711.

Tong, K., Dubé, C., & Sekuler, R. (2019). What makes a prototype a prototype? Averaging visual features in a sequence. *Attention, Perception, & Psychophysics*, *81*(6), 1962–1978.

Tong, K., Ji, L., Chen, W., & Fu, X. (2015). Unstable mean context causes sensitivity loss and biased estimation of variability. *Journal of Vision*, *15*(4), 15.

Torralba, A., Oliva, A., Castelhano, M. S., & Henderson, J. M. (2006). Contextual guidance of eye movements and attention in real-world scenes: the role of global features in object search. *Psychological Review*, *113*(4), 766–786.

Treisman, A. (2006). How the deployment of attention determines what we see. *Visual Cognition*, *14*(4–8), 411–443.

Treisman, A. M., & Gelade, G. (1980). A feature integration theory of attention. *Cognitive Psychology*, *12*(1), 97–136.

Treisman, A., & Gormican, S. (1988). Feature analysis in early vision: evidence from search asymmetries. *Psychological Review*, *95*(1), 15–48.

Treue, S., Hol, K., & Rauber H. J. (2000). Seeing multiple directions of motion—Physiology and psychophysics. *Nature Neuroscience*, 3, 270–276.

Utochkin, I. S., & Brady, T. F. (2020). Individual representations in visual working memory inherit ensemble properties. *Journal of Experimental Psychology: Human Perception and Performance*, *46*(5), 458–473.

Utochkin, I. S., & Tiurina, N. A. (2014). Parallel averaging of size is possible but range-limited: A reply to Marchant, Simons, and De Fockert. *Acta Psychologica*, *146*, 7–18.

Utochkin, I. S., & Vostrikov, K. O. (2017). The numerosity and mean size of multiple objects are perceived independently and in parallel. *PloS One*, *12*(9), e0185452.

Utochkin, I. S. (2015). Ensemble summary statistics as a basis for rapid visual categorization. *Journal of Vision*, *15*(8), 1–14.

Utochkin, I.S., Choi, J., & Chong, S.C. (2022). A population response model of ensemble coding. bioRxiv. www.biorxiv.org/content/10.1101/2022.01.19.476 871v1.

Utochkin, I. S., Khvostov, V. A., & Stakina Y. M. (2018). Continuous to discrete: Ensemble-based segmentation in the perception of multiple feature conjunctions. *Cognition*, *179*, 178–191.

Utochkin, I. S., & Yurevich, M. A. (2016). Similarity and heterogeneity effects in visual search are mediated by "segmentability". *Journal of Experimental Psychology: Human Perception and Performance, 42* (7), 995–1007.

Verghese, P., & Stone, L. S. (1996). Perceived visual speed constrained by image segmentation. *Nature, 381*(6578), 161–163.

Virtanen, L. S., Olkkonen, M., & Saarela, T. P. (2020). Color ensembles: Sampling and averaging spatial hue distributions. *Journal of Vision, 20*(5), 1–14.

Vogel, E. K., & Machizawa, M. G. (2004). Neural activity predicts individual differences in visual working memory capacity. *Nature, 428*(6984), 748–751.

Vul, E., & Pashler, H. (2008). Measuring the crowd within: Probabilistic representations within individuals. *Psychological Science, 19*, 645–647.

Walker, D., & Vul, E. (2014). Hierarchical encoding makes individuals in a group seem more attractive. *Psychological Science, 25*(1), 230–235.

Ward, E. J., Bear, A., & Scholl, B. J. (2016). Can you perceive ensembles without perceiving individuals?: The role of statistical perception in determining whether awareness overflows access. *Cognition*, 152, 78–86.

Watamaniuk, S. N., & Duchon, A. (1992). The human visual system averages speed information. *Vision Research, 32*(5), 931–941.

Watamaniuk, S. N., & Sekuler, R. (1992). Temporal and spatial integration in dynamic random-dot stimuli. *Vision Research, 32*(12), 2341–2347.

Watamaniuk, S. N. J., Sekuler, R., & Williams, D. W. (1989). Direction perception in complex dynamic displays: The integration of direction information. *Vision Research, 29*(1), 47–59.

Webster, J., Kay, P., & Webster, M. A. (2014). Perceiving the average hue of color arrays. *Journal of the Optical Society of America, 31*(4), A283–A292.

Weiss, D. J., & Anderson, N. H. (1969). Subjective averaging of length with serial presentation. *Journal of Experimental Psychology, 82*(1, Pt.1), 52–63.

Wertheimer, M. (1923). Laws of organization in perceptual forms. In *A Source Book of Gestalt Psychology* (ed W. D. Ellis) (pp. 71–88). Kegan Paul, Trench, Trubner & Co.

Whiting, B. F., & Oriet, C. (2011) Rapid averaging? Not so fast! *Psychonomic Bulletin & Review, 18*, 484–489.

Whitney, D., & Yamanashi Leib, A. (2018). Ensemble perception. *Annual Review of Psychology, 69*, 105–129.

Wilken, P., & Ma, W. J. (2004). A detection theory account of change detection. *Journal of vision, 4*(12), 1120–1135.

Williams, R. S., Pratt, J., Ferber, S., & Cant, J. S. (2021). Tuning the ensemble: Incidental skewing of the perceptual average through memory-driven selection. *Journal of Experimental Psychology: Human Perception and Performance, 47*(5), 648–661.

Williams, D. W., & Sekuler, R. (1984). Coherent global motion percepts from stochastic local motions. *Vision Research, 24*(1), 55–62.

Wolfe, B. A., Kosovicheva, A. A., Leib, A. Y., Wood, K., & Whitney, D. (2015). Foveal input is not required for perception of crowd facial expression. *Journal of Vision*, *15*(4), 11.

Wolfe, J. M., Horowitz, T. S., & Kenner, N. M. (2005). Rare items often missed in visual searches. *Nature*, *435*(7041), 439–440.

Woodworth, R. S. (1938). Experimental psychology. New York: Holt.

Yamanashi Leib, A., Chang, K., Xia, Y., Peng, A., & Whitney, D. (2020). Fleeting impressions of economic value via summary statistical representations. *Journal of Experimental Psychology: General*, *149*(10), 1811–1822.

Yamanashi Leib, A., Fischer, J. T., Liu, Y. et al. (2014). Ensemble crowd perception: A viewpoint-invariant mechanism to represent average crowd identity. *Journal of Vision*, *14*(8), 26, 1–13.

Yamanashi Leib, A., Kosovicheva, A., & Whitney, D. (2016). Fast ensemble representations for abstract visual impressions. *Nature Communications*, *7*, 13186.

Yamanashi Leib, A., Landau, A. N., Baek, Y., Chong, S. C., & Robertson, L. (2012). Extracting the mean size across the visual field in patients with mild, chronic unilateral neglect. *Frontiers in Human Neuroscience*, *6*, 267.

Yang, F., Harrison, L. T., Rensink, R. A., Franconeri, S. L., & Chang, R. (2018). Correlation judgment and visualization features: A comparative study. *IEEE Transactions on Visualization and Computer Graphics*, *25*(3), 1474–1488.

Yang, Y., Tokita, M., & Ishiguchi, A. (2018). Is there a common summary statistical process for representing the mean and variance? A study using illustrations of familiar items. *i-Perception*, *9*(1), 2041669517747297.

Yantis, S., & Abrams, R. A. (2014). *Sensation and Perception*. New York: Worth.

Yildirim, I., Öğreden, O., & Boduroglu, A. (2018). Impact of spatial grouping on mean size estimation. *Attention, Perception, & Psychophysics*, *80*(7), 1847–1862.

Yörük, H., & Boduroglu, A. (2020). Feature-specificity in visual statistical summary processing. *Attention, Perception, & Psychophysics*, *82*(2), 852–864.

Yuan, L., Haroz, S., & Franconeri, S. (2019). Perceptual proxies for extracting averages in data visualizations. *Psychonomic Bulletin & Review*, *26*(2), 669–676.

Zepp, J., Dubé, C., & Melcher, D. (2021). A direct comparison of central tendency recall and temporal integration in the successive field iconic memory task. *Attention, Perception, & Psychophysics*, *83*(3), 1337–1356.

Zosh, J. M., Halberda, J., & Feigenson, L. (2011). Memory for multiple visual ensembles in infancy. *Journal of Experimental Psychology: General*, *140*(2), 141.

This review is dedicated to the memory of Mrs. Lily Safra, a great supporter of brain research

Funding Statement

SH was supported by a grant from the Israel Science Foundation (ISF)

Cambridge Elements

Perception

James T. Enns
The University of British Columbia

Editor James T. Enns is Professor at the University of British Columbia, where he researches the interaction of perception, attention, emotion, and social factors. He has previously been Editor of the *Journal of Experimental Psychology: Human Perception and Performance* and an Associate Editor at *Psychological Science, Consciousness and Cognition, Attention Perception & Psychophysics,* and *Visual Cognition.*

About the Series
The modern study of human perception includes event perception, bidirectional influences between perception and action, music, language, the integration of the senses, human action observation, and the important roles of emotion, motivation, and social factors. Each Element in the series combines authoritative literature reviews of foundational topics with forward-looking presentations of the recent developments on a given topic.

Cambridge Elements ☰

Perception

Printed in the United States
by Baker & Taylor Publisher Services